Leaving the 99

Forsaking Religion for the Treasure of Heaven

Alan Caplin

Leaving the 99
Copyright © 2023 by Alan Caplin
All rights reserved.

No part of this work may be reproduced, stored in a retrieval system, or transmitted in any form or by any means, electronic, mechanical, photocopying, or otherwise, without the prior written consent of the publisher. Short extracts may be used for review purposes.

Scripture quotations unless noted otherwise are taken from The ESV® Bible (The Holy Bible, English Standard Version®), copyright © 2001 by Crossway, a publishing ministry of Good News Publishers. Used by permission. All rights reserved.

Please visit **www.firelightministries.com** for additional ministry information.

I'd like to dedicate this book to my wife Lori, and every other friend of God who has cheered me on, prayed for me, spoken His own words over me, and lifted my arms when exhausted. You guys and gals know who you are, thank you.

Leaving the known for the unknown is never easy nor a straight path. Without your love, kindness, and support - none of what is written within these pages would have been possible.

I love you all, very much.

Table of Contents

The Parable .... Page 1

The Leaving .... Page 5

Counting the Cost .... Page 12

You Died! .... Page 18

Stay in Bed (Rest) .... Page 24

Finding Purpose .... Page 32

The Sovereignty of God .... Page 39

Growing into Maturity .... Page 48

Seeking His Righteousness .... Page 58

Covenant Promises .... Page 68

Eternal Security .... Page 78

A Living Sacrifice .... Page 94

The Two Anointings (Within and Upon) .... Page 101

Elijah and The Double Portion .... Page 113

Universalism and Preterism .... Page 122

Rapture Doctrine .... Page 133

Encouragement .... Page 141

Closing Prayer and Blessing .... Page 144

Introduction

In this season, The Lord is shaking the hearts of His people in order to bring mass transformation into the image (soul) of Jesus (2 Corinthians 3:18; Romans 8:29). The Lord is building an end time army, the hearts of sons and daughters are being shook in order to begin the fulfillment of great revival, harvest, and nations coming to Jesus (Isaiah 61:1-11; Zephaniah Ch 3; Joel Ch 3; Hebrews 12:26-29).

By *faith*, the heart of the believer contains the very presence of Christ (Ephesians 3:16-19), and from our inner being (belly) all we do flows directly through the heart (Proverbs 4:23; Proverbs 20:27).

Truly, things will continue to shake all around us until the hearts of His own people are **unshakeable**. Yes, what will **remain** within the hearts of this new army ... will be ***THE unshakeable*** ... that of The Spirit.

For those willing to boldly leave the certainty and stability of the *99* for the promises and unknown of the *1* - The Lord is paving the way for much power to flow through His sons and daughters. Just like Noah's Ark that came to rest upon a mountaintop, The Lord is shaping and preparing the heart of man to be the **unshakeable** resting place for the depths and power of His own Spirit (Psalm 125:1).

We are entering a place in time where those who desire surrender, self-sacrifice, and the fullness of The Lord ... will see rapid growth into great power of The Spirit.

These powerful servants of The Lord from across the globe will come into focus seemingly from nowhere. Coming out of sheer obscurity, these relatively unknown believers have trained and quietly prepared for years outside of the public view. These powerful "agents of righteousness" will be: of all ages; from all types of secular backgrounds; hungry for more of God and seeking the kingdom at any cost; and a balanced doctrinal teaching will emerge.

For too long most popular Christian teaching has focused on *either* God's kindness *or* God's severity ... when The Lord is in fact both.

"Note then the kindness and the severity of God: severity toward those who have fallen, but God's kindness to you, provided you continue in his kindness. Otherwise you too will be cut off." Romans 11:22

This focus on one extreme attribute of God at the expense of the other has brought into the church deceptiveness in the form of **legalism** (rules, performance based works, tradition, religiosity, and self-righteousness) and **false gracism** (all are saved, The Lord does everything for us without our participation, no obedience to The Lord is necessary, no judgment here or in eternity, no devil, no hell, et cetera).

Yet, in this new season, teaching will come from the middle place that honors both of these extreme attributes of God – His kindness and His severity. In that new balanced ground of doctrinal teaching, the *double portion inheritance* will come to the forefront. As sons and daughters, the double portion inheritance will bring great supernatural riches and our full inheritance in Christ.

Friends, the massive power coming upon the normal, every day believer, will shake the earth and the heart of man ... and nations will come to Jesus.

Alan Caplin

The Parable

"What do you think? If a man has a hundred sheep, and one of them has gone astray, does he not leave the ninety-nine on the mountains and go in search of the one that went astray?" Matthew 18:12

At first glance, the parable of the lost sheep would imply that pastors as the shepherd of the flock are, at times, to leave the sheep to go find the one that is lost. This would be the traditional view, and it's absolutely true! No doubt!

But, like with *all* scripture there can be so many deep, rich, and subtle layers of Truth that sadly go unnoticed.

To begin unveiling the heart of The Father within this parable, we must first consider *who* Jesus is addressing ... the Pharisees. These are self-righteous legalists who love money more than the people they serve (Luke 16:14).

Simply put, these religious leaders aren't doing their job!

In fact, in Matthew 23:13-38, Jesus doesn't hold back on these guys and blatantly shares his perfect assessment of the Pharisees. Jesus calls out their religious hypocrisy, He calls out their hearts.

Repeatedly calling them hypocrites, Jesus powerfully tells the Pharisees that they are denying the people access to the kingdom of heaven ... a kingdom that out of pride and arrogance they themselves refuse to enter into. Jesus goes on telling these religious elite that they work to win a single convert only to turn that person into a child of hell who is twice their own evil and wickedness! Jesus

LEAVING THE 99

continues to call them hypocrites that love their gold and own giving *more* than the altar the gold is placed on.

Jesus doesn't back down and continues to hammer away at their vast religious hypocrisy by calling them out for following the rules of Torah on tithing yet neglecting "the weightier matters of the law: justice and mercy and faithfulness." Essentially, these stone hearted religious elect are giving to get from God, and yet unable to give their own people the goodness of God!

Jesus tells them that they are far more concerned with outward appearances than the heart within. He calls them out for being filled with greed and self-indulgence, and for outwardly trying to appear beautiful and righteous while on the inside they are filled with lawlessness (sin).

At this point in their tense interaction, I can only imagine the death stares, eye rolls, grumbles, and teeth grinding Jesus was receiving from this tightly wound group. Yet, just in case these tone-deaf religious leaders weren't fully grasping the obvious message, Jesus calls them serpents and a brood of vipers who, by their own hypocrisy, are condemned to hell.

Yes, *these* are the people Jesus calls out for not going after the one.

You see, for those pastors who truly love the people they serve, doing the right thing isn't hard. Yes, The Lord may have to remind us what to do in that moment ... but His perfect love makes our obedience easy.

However, I see "leaving the 99 for the 1" as a symbol of far more than just leaving many sheep for the one sheep.

Alan Caplin

This parable is also a symbol of that which we hold onto in fear of moving forward by the love and Spirit of God.

Far too often The Lord is wanting us to let go of the sure *thing*, easy *thing*, comfortable *thing*, popular *thing*, or the traditional *thing* for the *one* important *thing* in that season the Holy Spirit wants to teach us. Yes, the Pharisees had let pride, arrogance, and self-piety get between them and the plans of God.

These religious elite were simply unable to let go of their own way because they were too busy seeking glory from each other:

"How can you believe, when you receive glory from one another and do not seek the glory that comes from the only God?" John 5:44

Friends, this is what tradition, religiosity, and systemic faith will produce. Religious mindsets will never fail to perpetuate a need to fit in, when we are called to boldly stand out. As part of the human condition we want to be accepted, to be recognized or known, and to belong with others in this world – just look at the powerful influence of social media. Yet, we can't impact the world when we look just like the world!

In Matthew 15:14, Jesus appropriately calls the Pharisees "blind guides" because they knowingly lead others into the very same pit that they are in. Yet, many believers are allowing themselves to be led by persons in positions of leadership who really don't know any better than *they* do!

This is why our hearts must be sensitive to His leading, and we must be ready to move from what we *have* into what God wants to *give* us. Frankly, sometimes what He has to give us is far less glamorous or popular than what

LEAVING THE 99

we are leaving, but I can guarantee that what you receive by leaving in faith will be key to much *more* of what He has for you!

In essence, here is what all this stuff about the Pharisees boils down to. Whether it's a church, career, position in ministry, a city or town, an abusive relationship, false teaching, rigid theological constructs, poor behavior patterns, unhealthy life choices, spiritual immaturity, or even sometimes a family ... we cannot allow pride, fear, and the threat of rejection to limit what God wants to do in our lives. Any person, place, or thing that we choose to cling to when Jesus tells us to *go* will always be rooted in hypocrisy.

Our lips profess love and faith, but the actions of the heart are often corrupted by fear and a reliance on self. Again, condemning the hypocrisy of the Pharisees, Jesus quotes the prophet Isaiah:

"This people honors me with their lips, but their heart is far from me;" Matthew 15:8

I don't want to be that guy. I've left more people, places, and things than I can count in search of the *one* thing He has for me in that given moment. In each situation where I could have said "no" and safely kept the status quo - it would have been a loss for the kingdom.

My prayer is that this book gently pushes you out of your comfort zone to go after *your* God given one thing. Yes, my heart's desire is that in our time spent together we build up your theological insight into biblical matters you have always wondered about, as well as shaping a deeper, trusted confidence in Jesus, and Jesus *alone*.

Alan Caplin

The Leaving

In my journey with The Lord, I have become an expert at leaving people, places, and situations where my spiritual growth flat out depended upon the new shift taking place. Frankly, someone in your tomorrow is counting on you to grow and be better today! Yes, that *one*, needs you to be shifting to the deeper things of God.

Since first becoming a believer in 1992, I have had to make *many* difficult adjustments.

In receiving Jesus, I had to leave Judaism at the risk of losing my entire extended family. It wasn't easy, but I made that choice because there was no way for me to deny the Truth of His presence in my own life. Sadly, many Jewish families will conduct funerals for those relatives who choose to follow Jesus, and they will very much consider these believers in Jesus as forever dead to the entire family. Believe me when I tell you, I risked everything to be the person I am today.

Thankfully everything worked out with my family, but I will tell you, when you can tell your Jewish mother that you believe in *Jesus* ... you can tell a gentile anything! This is why I have no issue boldly sharing what The Lord teaches me, no matter whose feathers get ruffled.

Yes. I've done lots and lots of leaving including a pastoral position in a denomination where I just couldn't teach any longer their rigid doctrinal views. I saw too many people living confused, fearful, angry, and repressed within their own hearts and minds. In fact, I had to leave behind the ministerial credentials that I worked and studied hard for.

LEAVING THE 99

Not only have I left the realms of religion and legalism, I have also left extreme gracism (the kind of false grace that includes universalism, preterism, and the notion that we don't need to be obedient because Jesus was already obedient for us). I love *grace*, but not a fan of *false grace*.

Honestly, both the false grace and anti-religion crowds first began to leave *me* because I was both hungering and chasing after supernatural healing, the more of God (which I cover in chapter 13), the gifts of The Spirit, and a much deeper understanding of the scriptures to include judgment. To me, operating in His healing is the natural extension of His own grace and goodness. But, this "new Alan" seemingly rubbed many the wrong way because it challenged their own faith.

Yes, I have also left a few social media pages with very large followings and spheres of influence simply because it wasn't where I was supposed to be any longer. The Lord needed me to get *offline* and be face to face with His people to receive much ministerial skill and supernatural growth. In fact, this post COVID move away from online was the start of our house church ministry.

And, now, I am preparing to retire from my job of nearly 30 years as a public educator. Yes. It's been a really great career! I have been blessed to be very successful and well known in my school district. I could easily do this job at a high level for the kiddos another 15 years or more. **BUT**, I want the promises The Lord has personally given to me. For those weighty promises of His hold far more value to me than the career I have.

Leaving, yeah, I get it. With each move I have lost family, friends, popularity, titles, connections, influence, security, and even a clear path at times. But you know what? With each and every move made, one or two people chose to keep walking down the road *with* me because they had understood my vision. With each new shift and each act of trusted obedience ... my relationship with The Lord grew deeper and powerful insight was gained into those things needed for the *next* part of the journey.

Truly, I have never once looked back with regret. Never! In fact, many wanted to follow Jesus, but were conflicted with their own needs and desires. Yet, they had wanted to take care of other matters first. Jesus said to one of them:

"No one who puts his hand to the plow and looks back is fit for the kingdom of God." Luke 9:62

We can't look back. That's key. Jesus is saying to us that if you put your hand to the plow while looking backwards – you will *destroy* or *waste* the crop as you plow the field totally crooked! We become unfit for service because we are torn between the world and the kingdom of God ... we simply cannot serve two masters.

The disciples themselves *never* looked back.

I love the story of Peter and his friends fishing with Jesus in Luke chapter 5. Jesus takes them out in the boat, just a bit offshore. Yes, Jesus taught these guys *with* them from inside the boat, and then after the short kingdom teaching, Jesus demonstrated the Truth spoken by taking them to the deep waters where they were frustrated just before.

Suddenly, from an act of ***obedience to the direction and leading of The Lord***, the fishing nets were full and near bursting open! Even two fishing boats couldn't contain the entire haul.

Friends, we must allow The Lord to ***take*** us out into the

LEAVING THE 99

deep waters ***with*** Him where we are frustrated, stretched, and uncomfortable. Yes, this is most often the only place where the reality of true riches in Christ can be revealed.

Peter and his business partners understood that Jesus had for them far deeper and wider than the load of fish. Once Peter and his fishing friends got over to the shore, they had *immediately* left the boats and the haul of fish …. to follow the ***One***.

"And when they had brought their boats to land, they left everything and followed him." Luke 5:11

Yes! These guys could have taken all that fish and sold it for a pretty penny. These professional fishermen had full fishing nets and sudden wealth, but something was still missing. They'd have been set for a real long time with material wealth, but their hearts lacked fullness.

Although they understood little about the kingdom at that moment, they had stood incomplete without leaving it all behind for the ***One***. Their hearts knew. They knew where their true treasure was, it was in the Person of Jesus, not in the fish. As Jesus has said, "For where your treasure is, there your heart will be also." Matthew 6:21

When it comes to leaving for the sound of a voice, there is no greater biblical example than Abraham. Abram really had very little reason to leave his country. He had a wife named Sarai, and because of his father Terah's acquired wealth, Abram had very many possessions and a number of slaves (Genesis 12:4-6).

At 75 years old, Abram thought his life was pretty well complete, he had it good. Yet, he followed a voice to a place that would ***eventually*** be shown to him. Abram left everything that he had ever known for the promise of a blessing! Yes! He left it all for the unknown!

Now the LORD said to Abram, "Go from your country and your kindred and your father's house to the land that I will show you." Genesis 12:1

Yep, Abram didn't even know where he was going - he had no clue! He just wanted what the voice had for him, Abram wanted the blessing more than he wanted to stay in his comfort zone. Friends, we don't ever *need* to know where we are going in order to leave a place that now sits in a different season.

Fast forward 24 years, Abram was 99 years old. He still had not obtained the promise of a son who would be his eventual heir to all that he had (Genesis 25:5). Right here is where things get interesting about the number 99, this fries my brain!

"But I will establish my covenant with Isaac, whom Sarah shall bear to you at this time next year." Genesis 17:21

Yep, at 99 years old The Lord now renames Abram to Abraham (as a mark of covenantal transition **_with_** The Lord) and promises the birth of Isaac one full calendar year later ... at 100 years old!

The number 99 is literally a number of spiritual transition from the promises of The Lord having been seeded to the promises becoming manifest! 99 as a number, is a place of being content, but not being complete! The transition in our walk from 99 to 100 is the revealing of that which has been concealed in order to receive the fullness of the promises of God!

LEAVING THE 99

This is exactly why we cannot settle for the false safety of 99, we must make the uncomfortable journey to 100!!

Remember, in the parable of the sower Jesus speaks of the seed (word of God and His given promises) that take root within the healthy soil (heart of man):

"But those that were sown on the good soil are the ones who hear the word and accept it and bear fruit, thirtyfold and sixtyfold and a hundredfold." Mark 4:20

Yes!!!! Hundredfold is the fullness of the heart, it is **HIS** fruit of the Spirit coming out from within *your* new heart (Ezekiel 36:26). The number 100, as a measure, is simply the fullness of his own seed (word) blooming within you! Friends, to *not* transition from 99 to 100 is to leave some of His goodness on the table of righteousness, and I want to receive all He has for me.

What's more, is that the number 100 also symbolizes the fullness or completeness of our reward for leaving it all behind!! Peter "complains" to Jesus how they have left everything behind and followed him (Mark 10:29), and Jesus said to him:

"Truly, I say to you, there is no one who has left house or brothers or sisters or mother or father or children or lands, for my sake and for the gospel, who will not receive a hundredfold now in this time" Mark 10:29-30

Leaving the 99 in faith for the 1, is to receive the fullness of all He has for us, both here and in eternity. But, let me throw this yellow caution flag at you. We are not to leave any person, place, or thing based on our own emotion, but rather on the leading of the Spirit. Just because we might

Alan Caplin

feel frustrated, angry, taken for granted, or totally worn out aren't reasons to up and leave the 99.

Those very real emotions are the reasons to start inquiring with God. Why? Because emotions do not equal the Holy Spirit. Emotions can be chemical, situational, reactionary, short sighted, fear based, triggered or trauma induced, and generated by our own thinking. Emotions are products of the flesh and will absolutely bring death. Yet, the other is Spirit and brings life, hope, and peace.

Emotions are good ... for there is *no* free will without them. Imagine going to a wedding or funeral, or watching your favorite baseball team win the World Series, or seeing the birth of your child and feeling nothing! Emotions are sheer proof that you *do* have free will!

Like the check engine warning lights in a car, emotions are good because they are indicators to take a look under the hood. We must look at the root cause of negative emoting or bad believing, and bring those raw issues before "The Great Mechanic" in order to help us straighten out our thinking.

In reality, that's all renewing the mind means. By the Spirit of God we take our crooked thoughts and horrid believing straight to The Lord, and have God help us align ourselves with what is *actually* true!

Friends, please be led. Be led to amazing new places. Be led to your *one* thing in The Lord. But we aren't ever to be led by our human emoting and feeling, we are led by His Spirit and knowing.

LEAVING THE 99

Counting the Cost

Most believers get enough of the gospel to be saved, but not enough of Truth to be free from themselves and the world. In fact, religion itself teaches us how to keep the front yard mowed, while doing little for the inside of the house. Yes, we know how to put up a good front and look great on the outside ... while we are rotting and decaying on the inside.

Religion tells you *what* to do, but when you know *who* you are, you will know *what* to do! This is why my goal for the rest of this book is to teach you just that ... who you are and what that means for *you* going forward. Being led by God is easy once you truly understand the gospel, your role here in the earth, and the supernatural riches the gospel contains.

In the parable of the sower, Jesus tells us that the key to bearing fruit and a healthy crop, is for the heart (soil) to hear the message of the word (seed) and to **_understand_** it:

"As for what was sown on good soil, this is the one who hears the word and understands it. He indeed bears fruit and yields, in one case a hundredfold, in another sixty, and in another thirty." Matthew 13:23

Religion uses an iron fist teaching a mixed message of law and grace that sadly combines our measured performance with His own goodness. This, in my opinion, is the reason legalism burns out their constituents. This mixed message makes it near impossible for followers of Jesus to produce a consistent and lasting crop from their **hearts**!

Alan Caplin

Unfortunately, many believers who leave religion have been so badly wounded by the "systemic church" that they don't want to hear about the cost of being a disciple of Jesus. In fact, many will adamantly say that there are *no* disciples of Jesus on this side of the cross. Please remember, we can be so *opposed* to something, that we fail to be *for* something!

I've had many people over the years tell me that there aren't disciples on this side of the cross because the cost is *too* high. This makes me very sad for them because without a surrendered cost - aside from eternal salvation upon belief - there is little inheritance to receive *here* in the earth.

Friends, the cost of being a disciple of Jesus, is *the* key to understanding the riches contained within the gospel. Our Father has left us a legal will or inheritance of riches upon the death, burial, resurrection, and ascension of His Son. To receive the contents of the will, we must first understand the riches from a lens of obedience and a cost of participation.

Before I get into the cost of being a disciple of Jesus, I want to tell you how much God loves you. I want to powerfully show you *why* Jesus *stayed* nailed to the cross, as He could have easily jumped down ... but love for us kept Him there.

"Love the Lord your God with all your heart and with all your soul and with all your mind." Matthew 22:37

Jesus is quoting Deuteronomy 6:5, this is the requirement of *how* to love The Lord under *the law*. Without the Lord, this just isn't possible for *us* to do.

LEAVING THE 99

If this was The Lord's specific expectation of love under the system of law ... then Jesus loves **_us_** His own creation that way! What's not possible for us, is the very standard of what's more than possible for God. The Lord, as love and righteousness, cannot morally ask us to do something that He Himself *cannot* do!

Jesus loves us with every single fiber of His being. And, we now get to love others the same way that He loves us, with our entire heart and from a place of selflessness.

"A new commandment I give to you, that you love one another: just as I have loved you, you also are to love one another." John 13:34

Friends, selflessness flowing from love has a cost. And, the cost is *you*.

Jesus said to the Jews who had believed him, "If you abide in my word, you are truly my disciples, and you will know the truth, and the truth will set you free." John 8:31-32

Jesus tells us what it takes to be a disciple, if we abide (or remain like bone) in both the written and living word, we are His disciples. And knowing the truth of the word, will set us free.

Catch that! Many who bitterly leave religion want to say this verse was spoken only to the Jewish people who had believed and therefore it isn't applicable to us. Well, then there is no way for us to be free!

Why? Because Jesus is saying that abiding or remaining in Him, and intimately knowing Jesus ... sets us free. Yes, the Truth that brings freedom can only be understood from our abiding or staying in Jesus! If you believe in Jesus, you are to be a disciple ... just like the original twelve.

Yet, the cost is yourself and all that you are.

In Luke 14:25-33, Jesus blows my mind as He spells out the cost of discipleship. He tells us to carry our own cross (our purpose in the earth) and to come after Him. He goes on to tell us that nobody builds a tower without first figuring out the cost. Why? Because that builder will look foolish and be mocked when they don't have enough funds or materials to complete the massive project. Jesus then goes on to give the example of kings going to war, but first figuring out if they have enough troops to go head-to-head with the other army. If the king sees off in the distance they are outnumbered, he will quickly send a delegation to figure out terms for peace.

Jesus **then** says, *"So therefore, any one of you who does not renounce all that he has cannot be my disciple." Luke 14:33*

Whoa! I have to renounce everything to be His disciple? Yes, because under the new covenant (His last will and testament) you have _full_ access by faith to all that **He** has! What Jesus has at His very disposal is ours, and what we have at our disposal is now His. By covenant, Jesus gives us His strength, abilities, and resources and takes on our weaknesses, perceived lack, and limitations. He gives us His faith (Hebrews 12:2), and we give Him our fear!

Jesus is saying we must come to the end of self. We must come to the end of our own resources and abilities to get things done. Instead, we must begin through faith to build the kingdom of God *"foolishly"* with His resources and abilities! Friends, Jesus is saying to us that if the dream sitting within your heart is inside your own resources and

LEAVING THE 99

what seems to be obtainable ... your long-term ministerial vision or expectation isn't big enough.

True surrender and selflessness comes at that place of where nothing you can do is of your *own* accord. Yes, the real cost of being a disciple of Jesus is any reliance on self. In fact, I would say that fear is really nothing more than an outward manifestation of a reliance on self. Simply put, fear breaks off when reliance is shifted from oneself to Jesus. Our 'yes' to Him isn't at all dependent upon us ... we don't respond to our ability, we respond to His ability!

What's impossible by the flesh, is possible by the Spirit! The flesh isn't your reality, the spirit is! If Jesus says it is true, then no matter what you see with your eyes, it's true!

Jesus tells us that the kingdom of heaven is a treasure to be sought after - and once it's found - everything is sold with great joy in order to buy and work that field. Truly, leaving the 99 for the 1 is the laser focus of the heart to go find that field of treasure that's been hidden from our sight. Friends, we can't *find* the treasure if we stay content where we are.

"The kingdom of heaven is like treasure hidden in a field, which a man found and covered up. Then in his joy he goes and sells all that he has and buys that field."
Matthew 13:44

Much the same, Jesus makes the distinct parallel between the kingdom of heaven and fine pearls:

"Again, the kingdom of heaven is like a merchant in search of fine pearls, who, on finding one pearl of great value, went and sold all that he had and bought it."
Matthew 13:45-46

Alan Caplin

There is a cost to finding the treasure of heaven. Again, that cost is to shift the focus from self and to place our full gaze upon Jesus.

Recently, I bought a new wedding ring – after 31 years of marriage I thought it would be really neat to go get a new ring as a symbol of our continued journey together. So, I had a ring custom made with fine pearls in it – to me it was a symbol of leaving everything rooted in self for both my wife and Jesus.

Well, a few days later, my wife, without knowing what I had actually picked out, sent me a text. The text read:

"You are the pearl of great price, and Father sold all that He had to purchase you. You are the treasure in the field, and He came into this world and found you. Never doubt His love or allow its fire to dim within your heart. He continues to stir up your heart so that you will know His great love for you and experience His endless delight in you." ~ Lori Caplin

Yes. I still cry reading that.

Jesus loves you so much that He gave all He had, sought you out, and purchased you. **YOU** are His treasure in the field, and so too is the 1 that you are assigned to go after. Never give up, never give in, and never let the precious flame go out within you. Allow The Lord to stir up your heart, and to show off His selfless love through you to others.

LEAVING THE 99

You Died!

The last few years here in the United States and around the globe, The Lord has been moving powerfully through His people. Revival is everywhere, it doesn't take much to see the rapid growth of deliverance and healing ministries. In fact, with so much power on display, many cessationists have had to stop and reconsider their views.

Yet, for me anyway, here is the thing. I do not believe The Lord is reviving a dead, old, broken religious system that never really worked for the people in the first place. Yes, The Lord is moving to bring in the lost, breathing new life into the tired, reviving ministries that were stumbling, and waking up those believers who sat dormant ... but we are really sitting in a season of massive reform for the church.

No longer will the believer be held under the bondage of self and be asked to carry the burden of impossible yokes established by systemic religion. Instead, reformation has come to move the church into her powerful destiny. That great destiny is one where each and every believer will be given the opportunity to walk this earth like Jesus did ... in love, selflessness, and great power.

I'm highly opposed to the burden of religion, but I'm more opposed to the burden of self. As another reformation of the church has come, we must obtain a better understanding of what healthy doctrine looks like and how that proper view of the gospel frees us from our self-imposed burdens.

All theological structures must have a solid and sound base to build teaching upon. Just like when you build a building, if the foundation isn't straight and solid, the structure itself will eventually have issues and crumble. In my view, any theological teaching must be **built** upon this foundation:

Paul writes, *"Do you not know that all of us who have been baptized into Christ Jesus were baptized into his death?"* Romans 6:3

To me, our co-death is the very epicenter of the gospel. If we never understand our death at the cross, we will never learn how to be alive here and now.

Here is a little insight to what baptism *(baptizō)* looked like in the first century. The Jewish people would take cloth and prepare it for use by dipping it into bleach, and then dipping the cloth into a color dye. Yes, the word baptism is really a nifty word for immersion.

Having first been immersed into the bleach, the cloth had all its filth and impurities fully stripped away. This immersion into the bleach created a base layer in order to give the new color dye something to fully adhere to. Once the bleached cloth was immersed into the new color, the cloth itself took on a brand new identity as either red, purple, yellow, green, et cetera.

Yes, this is what first century believers had understood as a baptism. We are immersed as one entity, and come out fully prepared to be immersed *again* into our new and **permanent** color form – transformed as a new creation.

Those who, at belief from the heart, have been baptized *into* Christ Jesus, were also baptized *into* His death. Yes the very moment we believe in Jesus, we are first immersed into His own death, and then immersed into the living Christ - made *alive* together in the here, now, and the forever (Colossians 2:13; Ephesians 2:5; Philippians 2:1; 1 Corinthians 6:17).

LEAVING THE 99

Yes, you and I as believers have died with Him at the cross, been perfectly hidden and tucked away forever *in* covenant with Jesus, and await the purpose of our lives to be revealed in Christ (Colossians 3:3).

Like the cloth immersed into the bleach, our *old selves* have been neutralized by being immersed into death – and our *new selves* have been made alive by immersion into Jesus. Our flesh and our way died at the cross, and with it our old ways of thinking, being, problem solving, communicating, and relating to others.

As believers, we have been freely given the mind, wisdom, clarity, and instruction of Christ, and yes access to His very own thoughts by His own Spirit (1 Corinthians Chapter 2).

You and I have **risen** with Him out of the waters of death as a new creation, and are no longer guided in this world with our fleshly minds, lusts, and passions … but rather with a *fused* Spirit of both His and ours (Colossians 2:12-13 and Romans 8:14-16).

In essence, water baptism is an amazing representation of what happened upon belief from our heart (Romans 10:10). We are immersed into the waters of death *with* Jesus, and then we come up *out* of the waters into the air of life to be made *alive with* Jesus. It's such a powerful visualization of both death and life, so blatantly vivid that once I understood what the water baptism meant – I did it ***again***!

Water baptism for me means I died, and I no longer rely on me, rather I rely on the One who made me alive. Yet, we must come away from this "baptism of belief" identifying ourselves with the new creation in Christ, and not with the dead old man. As a brand new, gorgeous purple dress, we must learn to stop fighting our own maker and demanding

Alan Caplin

that we are a hideous swamp gas green! You are His child, co-heir to a kingdom, holy, eternal, sealed, a royal priest, forever fused with Him as One, righteous, and redeemed.

"For you died" - Colossians 3:3. It's just a basic fact. The old you died, the new you lives in Christ.

"For one who has died has been set free from sin." Romans 6:7

Dead people don't worry, want, need, complain, argue, talk back, ask questions, negotiate with evil, or ***sin***. Why? They are too busy being about The Father's business.

You died. You have been *forever* made alive. And you are alive in covenant with Christ to bear fruit for the kingdom. Those who are dead to the old self, and alive in the new self are able to fully draw upon His grace.

As I've written previously, we must learn to come to a full reliance on ***Jesus*** and not on *self*. This is why understanding our death of the old man (fallen human nature) at the cross is so powerful.

When you join the army, you don't buy your own gear. The army itself supplies you with all you need for your mission. Grace too is full supply. Truly, dead people don't provide for *themselves* - everything needed to bear fruit for Jesus is freely provided, by *faith*. But if we operate from any place outside of our co-death and reliance on Him, The Lord on some level literally opposes us.

But he gives more grace. Therefore it says, "God opposes the proud but gives grace to the humble." James 4:6

LEAVING THE 99

If you think *you* provide for *you*. Well. That's pride! Truly, to receive the free provision of His grace and goodness, we must flow in humility out of the new self. Yes, we must first embrace our death to fully and freely live out our call as the new creation.

Friends, the more we understand and live from our death at the cross, the more fruit will hang from our limbs. And, the more peace, favor, provision, and joy you will walk in.

Truly, the disciples themselves were transformed from big time fraidy cats to bold and courageous kingdom shakers when they finally *understood* the cross. When they finally realized **who** they were, **who** they belonged to, and **who** they were purposed for ... nothing was more important than spreading the Truth about Jesus, hope, joy, and goodness.

Yet, this transformation came despite the cost of their own lives. True transformation in our walk comes from realizing that your limited time here on earth isn't about you! Nope, it's about the kingdom.

Yes, realizing that you've already died *once*, and will never die again. You read that right! You will one day experience a physical death to your body, but by the Spirit you are alive here, now! Friends, you don't die physically and then live *again* in heaven. You are born again, now! Your body will one day fade while your eternal spirit *continues* to live on.

In fact, you *already* dwell in eternity!

"But our citizenship is in heaven, and from it we await a Savior, the Lord Jesus Christ, who will transform our lowly body to be like his glorious body, by the power that enables him even to subject all things to himself."
Philippians 3:20-21

Alan Caplin

You as a believer in Jesus Christ have a dual citizenship, one here on earth and one in heaven. Yes, you were first physically born in the earth, and then you were spiritually born (again) in heaven. Paul tells us that from **HEAVEN** *you* are awaiting the return of the The Lord Jesus Christ.

You died, you were made eternal and forever, and you no longer belong to yourself. Yes, after The Lord's return to earth you will receive a glorified body like Christ's ... but in the meantime you belong to The Lord to bear fruit, here.

"Likewise, my brothers, you also have died to the law through the body of Christ, so that you may belong to another, to him who has been raised from the dead, in order that we may bear fruit for God." Romans 7:4

As I continue to write, I'm giggling. Many of you are just now realizing I'm telling you that you cannot lose your eternal salvation, ever. I will cover this more in depth in a later chapter on eternal security. In that section, I will lay out more evidence on this critical Truth and I will dispel myths from the misinterpretation of scripture.

Yet, knowing that *you* can't mess up your own eternity, and knowing that *you* belong to another and are alive in Christ simply for the benefit of *others* .... will set you free from you. Why? When you are fully dead to you ... you are then finally free to be alive in Him. Friend, even on your very worst day, His Spirit still dwells in you. That's a guarantee.

Truly, the more dead you are to you, the more of Christ and His kingdom power that will flow through you. Sadly, too many say the cost is too high. I'd simply say a dead man has no need, no desire, and no time to resist the will of God.

You died. Rest in Peace (RIP).

LEAVING THE 99

Stay in Bed (Rest)

The Jewish people in biblical times had this notion that if you were wealthy, you were blessed by God for having been obedient with following the law and the commands of The Lord. Jesus encountered a young rich ruler who was very wealthy and followed *all* the commandments of the law ... with precision! This young man believed that he was blessed by God with wealth for his obedience and being "good."

Being pressed upon his heart to know, the young man then begins to sincerely ask Jesus how he can receive eternal life. Jesus responds:

"One thing you still lack. Sell all that you have and distribute to the poor, and you will have treasure in heaven; and come, follow me." But when he heard these things, he became very sad, for he was extremely rich." Luke 18:22-23

This young man wasn't able to leave the 99 for the **One**. This guy knew the law, but didn't know The Lord. This man had more trust in his wealth than in God. This young guy put his treasure in his bank account instead of in the things of God.

Truly, this guy had *everything*, but *nothing* at all!

This man was basically saying, "Jesus, you aren't enough for me." This shocked rich guy who thought he had it all figured out, "lacked **one** thing" ... the ability to **rest** in the promises of God.

Alan Caplin

To me, this is the single **_most_** important chapter in this entire book, for the biblical requirement of rest is where our hidden treasure comes from! Friends, **_this_** is how the promises of God become manifest from the unseen realm into the seen realm! Truthfully, there is no other way as we must live *from* His rest in order to receive.

"For who were those who heard and yet rebelled? Was it not all those who left Egypt led by Moses? And with whom was he provoked for forty years? Was it not with those who sinned, whose bodies fell in the wilderness? And to whom did he swear that they would not enter his rest, but to those who were disobedient? So we see that they were unable to enter because of unbelief."
Hebrews 3:16-19

The Israelites could not enter the promised land because they couldn't **_first_** enter into His rest. Their unbelief, and unbelief of the heart alone, had been counted by The Lord as disobedience and rebellion ... which blocked out their entrance into their promise of destiny (Hebrews 3:12).

"Therefore, while the promise of entering his rest still stands, let us fear lest any of you should seem to have failed to reach it." Hebrews 4:1

The author of Hebrews is telling us that as new covenant believers, we too have the promise of rest, and failing to reach that rest would be highly unproductive for entering into **_our_** promises of destiny. As a believer in Jesus, you have one job! Yes, you have one thing to *strive* for with each and every ounce of your flesh, strength, mind, heart, and will ... that's to sit at rest.

"Let us therefore strive to enter that rest, so that no one may fall by the same sort of disobedience." Hebrews 4:11

LEAVING THE 99

I wrote earlier about having died and resting in peace (RIP). This visual concept is literally what The Lord is asking us to do with the old man, the old self, the fallen human nature, and the flesh. You died, as a dead person you have no need of your own getting or figuring! Jesus has it, you RIP!

Now, I'm not saying The Lord won't provide for us when we are parked outside of His rest, He loves you and He is your provider. But, we must reach maturity in order to walk into the deep promises of His purpose, call, and destiny.

Yet, most believers don't really understand what **_REST_** is, so it cannot be properly obtained. Let's fix that!

The word rest in the Greek is katapausis ... yes, it's a noun! It's a person, place, or thing ... it is not a verb requiring an action. Rest is to believe (verb/action) _upon_ Jesus, who is both a Person and a Place. The Israelites failed to believe upon The Lord that The Lord _is_ enough! When we sit at rest, Jesus _is_ our supply! When we sit outside of rest, _we_ become our supply! Friends, the sabbath is no longer a day of the week, it's a Person! Yes, Jesus is the 8th day, _today_! Every day, _today_, Jesus **IS** our sabbath rest (Hebrews 4:4-10). Jesus and Jesus alone is our full peace and supply!

Friends, this is seriously the most important lesson that I can teach the body of Christ, especially in these times. Rest itself has two separate components, faith and trust: **Rest = Faith + Trust**

Faith and trust are inverted to each other, but do work together. **FAITH** is believing without actually having **SEEN** any evidence to support the belief.

"Now faith is the assurance of things hoped for, the conviction of things not seen." Hebrews 11:1

Alan Caplin

TRUST is believing despite having **SEEN NEGATIVE** evidence that would refute the stuff we are faithing for. We literally have to suspend our own understanding in favor of His understanding.

"Trust in the LORD with all your heart, and do not lean on your own understanding. In all your ways acknowledge him, and he will make straight your paths." Proverbs 3:5-6

Faith is for the **UNSEEN** promise. Trust is for the **SEEN** stuff that is trying to steal the yet unseen promise. Faith is freely given, it's a gift (Hebrews 12:2). Yet. Trust is both a choice and a response flowing out of our given faith.

"Those who trust in the Lord are like Mount Zion, which cannot be shaken but endures forever." Psalm 125:1

If God says to you, "Go to Uncle Fred's house and have him drive you 100 miles to the Florida State line. You will find what I have for you there." Your faith has been activated for that which you haven't yet seen.

You get to Fred's house and you see that Fred has a patch over his right eye, has 3 DUI's, he was released from jail last night, the car is all banged up, his breath reeks of alcohol, and the car's brakes aren't working that great.

You now have **MUCH** evidence to **REFUTE** faith for getting in the car with Fred. Your brain screams run!!!

You turn to The Lord and say, "Really? You *really* want me to do this?" He says, "Yes" ... and then you are asked to employ obedience with trust ... and still get in the car.

As you drive along with Fred, with each and every scary moment gone bye, you see God's loving goodness, His

LEAVING THE 99

protection, and you deeply come to realize that God has you at every corner. In what seems to be chaos, our faith grows. Intimacy grows. Love for Fred grows. Character grows. And Fred got to experience Jesus (yes, you) and got *saved* along the way.

In tough circumstances, trust is literally the suspension of our own understanding in order to gain the shalom peace of His perfect understanding. Yes, God joyfully gives us His own strength to operate in faith and trust. And, it's my experienced opinion that many promises go seemingly as failed .... because we don't both grasp and act upon this principle.

Look at it like this. If a cross country skier only uses one ski instead of the provided two skis ... they will fall down or go in circles. Yet, too much of the church is falling or just walking in chaotic circles because we are only using one ski!!!!

We ......

Faith
Trust
Faith
Trust
Faith
Trust

One ski after the other. Anything less is unbelief, and that makes us double minded, receiving nothing.

This is where Israel stumbled, The Lord desired them to return to Him in a place of surrendered trust. That place of deep trust was to *be* their strength. Instead they were stubborn and had wanted to make their own plans and do things their own way ... and to their demise, The Lord let them do it their own way!

For thus said the Lord GOD, the Holy One of Israel, "In returning and rest you shall be saved; in quietness and in trust shall be your strength." But you were unwilling.
Isaiah 30:15

I had a simple, powerful dream recently. I was asleep in bed (at my place of rest) and the lion who comes to steal, kill, and destroy took a bite out of the side of the mattress. He died, he was toast! He took a bite out of my place of rest, and he had nothing to sink his teeth into that would shake me and bring panic. Peace ruled and reigned!

But, I got out of bed to check on the lion. I pushed it, I poked at it, and moved it a little ... and he woke up, came back to life. The lion couldn't harm me, I could feel that! But, when I went to check on the devil, I left my place of rest in Jesus. Staying in that rest bed renders the devil powerless, getting out of bed (rest) gives him a foothold.

Friends, stay in bed! Please do keep your peace!

Rest is really aligning the thoughts of both the heart and mind with the Truth of who Jesus is as our provider. Yes, both the heart and mind think. The mind and heart are the two engines of the soul realm, both think consciously and subconsciously.

"For the word of God is living and active, sharper than any two-edged sword, piercing to the division of soul and of spirit, of joints and of marrow, and discerning the thoughts and intentions of the heart." Hebrews 4:12

The author of Hebrews, in the *same* section of scripture speaking of the importance of rest and single mindedness

LEAVING THE 99

... tells us that the word of God discerns the thoughts and intentions of the *heart*.

Yes, the heart thinks!

In the parable of the sower (Matthew 13:22), a sickly crop comes out from *within* the heart that has the seed (word of God) being choked out by "the cares of the world and the deceitfulness of riches." Yes, these thorns and thistles (thoughts and faulty belief sets) sit **inside** the heart!!!!

Yes, the heart thinks!

When Jesus perceived their thoughts, he answered them, "Why do you question in your hearts? Luke 5:22

But Jesus, knowing their thoughts, said, "Why do you think evil in your hearts? Matthew 9:4

Yes, the heart thinks!

"Now some of the scribes were sitting there, questioning in their hearts." Mark 2:6

Jesus said to them, "Why are you troubled, and why do doubts arise in your hearts?" Luke 24:38

"Mary treasured up all these things, pondering them in her heart." Luke 2:19

Yes, the heart thinks!

Friends, there's a big difference between a believing mind and a truly convinced heart. When the heart and mind are thinking different things, we are double minded or double souled. James tells us:

Alan Caplin

"For that person must not suppose that he will receive anything from the Lord; he is a double minded man, unstable in all his ways." James 1:7-8

Think for a moment about when you drive your car and hit a big pothole or curb. A tire or two gets badly jarred, and the car is now unable to go straight. Your front left tire is your mind and your front right tire is your heart.

When a bump in the road or large unexpected issue arises, both the heart and mind are subject to an impact. Unless we take the car into the shop for realignment of the two tires with the axle (Holy Spirit), the car will be unable to drive like it should. Getting to where you need to go, is now harder! Effective steering, is now hindered!

Friends, this is why we must guard our heart and renew the mind. This is the only way to stay at rest, keep peace, and to truly believe upon Jesus and Jesus **alone** for both the provision and manifestation of His promises.

"Guard your heart above all else, for it determines the course of your life." Proverbs 4:23

*"Do not be conformed to this world, but be transformed by the renewal of your mind, that by testing (**your thoughts**) you may discern what is the will of God, what is good and acceptable and perfect."* Romans 12:2 (**your thoughts** has been added by me for both clarity and emphasis)

Take your mind and heart into the shop as often as you can or need, "The Great Mechanic" longs to service your tires. Test your thoughts against the Truth of the written word and the Person of Jesus. Keep your peace, stay at rest, refuse to be rattled by demonic intimidation, and simply don't give the devil time or space to shake you from that core position of faith and trust.

LEAVING THE 99

Finding Purpose

"But we have this treasure in jars of clay, to show that the surpassing power belongs to God and not to us. We are afflicted in every way, but not crushed; perplexed, but not driven to despair; persecuted, but not forsaken: struck down, but not destroyed; always carrying in the body the death of Jesus, so that the life of Jesus may also be manifested in our bodies. For we who live are always being given over to death for Jesus' sake, so that the life of Jesus also may be manifested in our mortal flesh. So death is at work in us, but life in you."
2 Corinthians 4:7-12

My wife and I like to go for long walks in our neighborhood and my wife is kind enough to walk slow for me! Man, I'm getting old. Well, lately we have found ourselves picking up all the metal nails and screws that come across our path in the street. Truly, there are days we come across dozens of these things.

After meditating and praying about all these nails, I've come to realize that there are _3_ kinds of people in this world.

The **first** kind of person doesn't care a rats behind about the nails. They drop them. They let them fall out of their pick up or service trucks, they ignore them, they step over them. Frankly, they are aware of the nails. These people don't do dinky squat about them, even though the nails are a pest to everyone in the neighborhood.

Despite their lack of service to the community, it both rains and shines on these people and their families. Like everyone

Alan Caplin

else in the world, they experience both good things and bad things in their lives. And, usually, they thank themselves for the good stuff and find a way to blame God for all the bad stuff.

The **second** kind of person makes every effort to pick up the loose nails. They are good people, they love their neighbors. They do the *right* thing and are right standing (righteous) in their community. They pay close attention and serve. Why? Because it impacts people around them, and they take joy in loving others and helping people out.

Now, just because they do the right thing – and help people out – doesn't mean that they won't ever get a flat tire! They don't suddenly become immune to random flats from a well-placed metal object. They are in the world, and yes they are going to have to deal with worldly issues.

In fact, I can 100% guarantee that when they *do* get a flat tire … it will be an opportunity to advance the kingdom. I promise you, they will be a blessing, joy, inspiration, and point of witness to the dispatch operator, tow truck driver, and tire store guy.

Yes. Bad things happen to good people. Yet, bad junk will always be a kingdom growing opportunity … if we choose to operate our lives from that perspective.

The **third** kind of person … literally *takes* the nails for someone else.

The third kind of person sacrifices to advance the kingdom at all costs. The third kind of person knows who they are in Him and that they indeed belong to another (Romans 7:4). The third kind of person takes their suffering … and makes it meaningful to others.

LEAVING THE 99

The third kind of person knows they have a vast treasure deep inside them ... and that all they are is an earthenware vessel. The third kind of person knows they are a messenger of His love – and that their pain and troubles will one day be used to trouble the enemy.

The third kind of person shakes off the hurt that Jesus had promised would come – because He is right there in the storm with them. The third kind of person shakes off the dust to stand up and rise up for what is noble – and for what glorifies their King.

The third kind of person knows there is great purpose within them, because there is a great God dwelling inside of them. The third person understands that they have been given and entrusted with much, and that much more will be asked of them (Luke 12:48). The third person understands that the power of heaven dwells inside them (Ephesians 1:19-21), and they honor that deep understanding with great reverence and responsibility.

Friends, The Lord didn't design you to suffer. He designed you to walk with Him, to glorify Him, to be just like Him ... and to rule and reign with Him. You are royalty. Why? Because you are a child of *the* King. You are holy. Why? Because you are a child of *the* Holy One. You are a priest. Why? Because you are a child of *the* High Priest.

You were created for Him and greatly purposed by Him ... yep, flat tires and all. Truly, those who take the nails for others and plan *with* God for the good and growth of the kingdom ... there are heights, depths, and desires sitting within the heart itself that cannot even be searched in full.

Not only does God conceal things for kings to go search out (Proverbs 25:2), but those kings (sons) who are uncovering His

Alan Caplin

hidden treasure in the word ... have hearts themselves that are ***unsearchable.***

"As the heavens for height, and the earth for depth, so the heart of kings is unsearchable." Proverbs 25:3

As you search God, let God search ***you*** to bring out what only He can do! Yes, let Him pull out of your heart hidden treasure that only He can use to advance the kingdom in a unique way. And, what The Lord wants to do through His people is truly astonishing. Paul writes:

"To me, though I am the very least of all the saints, this grace was given, to preach to the Gentiles the unsearchable riches of Christ, and to bring to light for everyone what is the plan of the mystery hidden for ages in God, who created all things, so that through the church the manifold wisdom of God might now be made known to the rulers and authorities in the heavenly places." Ephesians 3:8-10

Friends, Paul is saying that the wisdom and plan of God is to bring to light for ***EVERYONE*** that ***THEY*** and ***YOU*** are called to show off Jesus to the rulers and authorities in the heavenly places! Yes, The Lord's plan or mystery is to give His sons and daughters great supernatural riches in order to show off the power of Jesus to ruling beings that sit in the heavens. In fact, Paul is saying ***this*** is the wisdom of God ... The Father thinks it's a ***great*** idea to show off Jesus, His Son, through you!

To take this mystery further, Jesus is the spirit realm ***head*** of the church. Many don't realize that the "Body of Christ" isn't a generic term referring to the group of people in the church organization or the numbers of members within the church itself. This term "Body of Christ" literally means that ***we*** are His spirit realm body. Jesus is the head over

LEAVING THE 99

every power and authority in heaven and earth, and His power and authority flows *through* the ***body of believers***!

Yes, you and I are His hands and feet, we do the work of Jesus attached to Him as the head of the body.

"For in him the whole fullness of deity dwells bodily, and you have been filled in him, who is the head of all rule and authority." Colossians 2:9-10

We are the **BODY** through which Jesus both speaks and acts! Imagine a picture of Jesus. Picture His head alone, then picture his entire body. The head is in charge of the whole body, and the rest of the body simply responds to the head. **WE** are that body, we do the work of Jesus, the head!

Track me here - King Jesus has ***all*** rule, power, authority, dominion, and has placed every name under ***HIS*** feet, not ***our*** feet.

"You made him for a little while lower than the angels; you have crowned him with glory and honor, putting everything in subjection under his feet." Hebrews 2:7-8

"And he put all things under his feet and gave him as head over all things to the church, which is his body, the fullness of him who fills all in all." Ephesians 1:22-23

Everything is under His feet. He is the head, you are **HIS BODY.** No matter what part of His body you are ... a toe, a finger nail, a hand, a foot, a belly button, or whatever ... **YOU** are now above every single power and authority in the heavens and earth!

As the spirit realm body of Jesus, as His pinky toe or His finger nail, **YOU** are so far above anything with a name!

Alan Caplin

Disease, cancer, death, sin, demonic, rulers, nature, and governmental agencies ... **YOU** in covenant with Jesus now sit in a higher realm and authority!

"and raised us up with him and seated us with him in the heavenly places in Christ Jesus, so that in the coming ages he might show the immeasurable riches of his grace in kindness toward us in Christ Jesus." Ephesians 2:6-7

Friends, when Jesus ascended, **YOU** ascended with Him! You, **RIGHT NOW**, sit in the lap of Christ and have His authority over all things in the heavens and earth. And, The Lord wants to show off His goodness, kindness, and the immeasurable riches of Christ, ***through*** you!

Truly, Jesus tells us to seek nothing but His kingdom, and that The Father **DESIRES** to give this kingdom to us!

"And do not seek what you are to eat and what you are to drink, nor be worried. For all the nations of the world seek after these things, and your Father knows that you need them. Instead, seek his kingdom, and these things will be added to you. "Fear not, little flock, for it is your Father's good pleasure to give you the kingdom." Luke 12:29-32

This is our purpose, to be just like Jesus in the earth! This is what The Father desires us to boldly seek after! This is what you were born (again) for!!

When we sow seeds into the ground of the earth, we expect the seed at full growth to look exactly like the picture on the package they came in. So, if we sow watermelon seeds, we expect watermelons to grow. If we sow sunflower seeds, we expect sunflowers to sprout up. If we sow pumpkin seeds, we expect pumpkins to grow. Simple!

LEAVING THE 99

The Son of Man (Jesus) continually sows seeds into the earth ... *"The one who sows the good seed is the Son of Man."* Matthew 13:37

But, who are the good seed?? The very next verse says ... *"The field is the world, and the good seed is the sons of the kingdom."* Matthew 13:38

When the ground of the heart is fertile, and the seed sown is nurtured, this good seed produces sons of God! Yes, we as believers are to look exactly like the picture on the package that the seeds came in.

This is why with every ounce of strength we have, we must strive or labor to enter into His rest. For the rest of Jesus, is the only way for us to look like Him. Living at this type of full surrender – exactly like Jesus did to The Father - is the only way to make Jesus our full supply.

You died, you rest in peace! Jesus does the heavy lifting as we walk surrendered in trusting obedience to His voice. Be that person, just like Jesus, who takes the nails for someone else. For, even greater shall you do!

"Truly, truly, I say to you, whoever believes in me will also do the works that I do; and greater works than these will he do, because I am going to the Father." John 14:12

Alan Caplin

The Sovereignty of God

There's lots of dangerous doctrine from within religion - most of which just makes people feel condemned, afraid, worthless, bitter, helpless, or even trapped. But there is no worse teaching than "selling" the idea that God is in 100% control of *all* that happens on the earth.

This teaching makes God out to be arbitrary and whimsical, and not a righteous judge or an arbitrator of *just* action. For God to allow sickness for this person and not for that one ... is a sick spiritual game of The Lord playing favorites with His children. Jesus doesn't love you or me any more or less than anyone else, so there must be deeper answers.

This view of God "allowing" sickness, creates 2 different *types* of God's we can believe in.

Type 1: An arbitrary, random, and inconsistent power who chooses to "allow" some to suffer and some to be whole, and every decision made is purely whimsical and based on fleeting fancy. This God is fickle, and favorites He does play. If you get close to this God, He **might** heal you. This God is both **bi-polar** and **ever-changing**.

Type 2: A loving, steady, unchanging power who refuses to renounce His gift of *__free will__* to mankind, and every single decision is made through His own tears and His merciful justice. You *can* get close to this God because He has **already** healed you, and while in the waiting for this healing to manifest ... we transform from victory to victory into an ever-increasing image of Jesus (Romans 8:29). There is no whimsy here, only love and justice!

LEAVING THE 99

Obviously, the *type 2* steady and unchanging God (Hebrews 13:8) is the God that we know and serve. But, the *type 1* bipolar, unreliable, and ever-changing view of God produces 2 counterproductive identities that manifest in the believer.

1) <u>**MARTYR**</u>: We get sick, bad things happen, or things go haywire in our lives – and we sit back in self-pity because this must be God's will for us. Many would say, "I'm just suffering for Jesus." Or, "I'm so glad that God gave me this cancer, many will come to The Lord through this." Or, "My faith hasn't been all that strong lately, and this must be to teach me a lesson - I need to be stronger."

2) <u>**VICTIM**</u>: Bad things happen and we blame God – "Why did **you** allow this!" Or, "How dare God let this happen to me. I'm furious at Him. I've been so faithful and this is the thanks I get."

In both identity scenarios, if God were human - the local child enforcement agency would come take the kids away!

Friends, God doesn't allow. God arbitrates justice.

Let's start here, "Sovereign Lord" biblically simply means Lord, Lord. Oxford's Online Dictionary defines the word *sovereignty* as "supreme power or authority" which puts The Lord in charge of all, but not in control of all.

Yes, The Lord is the supreme authority or highest power in all of the heavens and earth. The buck stops with Him, one day He will be fully accountable to <u>Himself</u> for there is no greater authority. He is in charge of all and yet has given us control over much. Yes. He could do everything for us, but that's not His will. He could micromanage us, that too is not His will.

Alan Caplin

The Lord's will is for us to have the gift of free will. God will never, ever touch our free will - because love itself is predicated on free will. If we aren't free to hate, we aren't free to love. Love is a choice. He wants us to choose Him from this place of love that isn't forced. Honestly, would you want your child or wife to love you because they **had** to?? Of course not. The Lord created us to share His love with us and through us from this ever-flowing fountain of free choice.

Yet, many say "free will" isn't a biblical term. Well, that is true. You won't find the term "free will" in the bible, but you will find in the bible the power of being able to make your own free choice.

"The good person out of the good treasure of his heart produces good, and the evil person out of his evil treasure produces evil, for out of the abundance of the heart his mouth speaks." Luke 6:45

"See, I have set before you today life and good, death and evil. If you obey the commandments of the LORD your God that I command you today, by loving the LORD your God, by walking in his ways, and by keeping his commandments and his statutes and his rules then you shall live and multiply, and the LORD your God will bless you in the land that you are entering to take possession of it. But if your heart turns away, and you will not hear, but are drawn away to worship other gods and serve them, I declare to you today, that you shall surely perish. You shall not live long in the land that you are going over the Jordan to enter and possess. I call heaven and earth to witness against you today, that I have set before you life and death, blessing and curse. Therefore choose life, that you and your offspring may live" Deuteronomy 30:15-19

LEAVING THE 99

Both in the Old Testament and in the New, there is the clear choice to follow His commands. Yes, we have the choice to let good or evil flow from deep within our own hearts. The covenants have changed, but His perfect ways of "choice" have not. We get to choose life or death: from Noah to Abraham to Moses to Jesus to the first disciples to us today – *this* has never changed.

Look, as the "Body of Christ" in covenant with Jesus, we have been given far more control than most people give us credit. But aside from free will, why else do troubles come?

- There is a god in this earth (the devil).
- There are demonic principalities.
- There are legal challenges by the accuser.
- There are fallen world issues, like our aging bodies.

Check this scenario out, (FW) means free will.

Jimmy is a believer (FW), but is constantly angry and bitter (FW) because his mom abandoned (FW) him when he was 5 years old. The anger and bitterness (FW) is causing his limbic system to be chemically out of whack (FW) - which has caused cancer (FW) to form in his body.

Because Jimmy has professed faith (FW) in Jesus - but holds such anger, resentment, bitterness, and unforgiveness (FW) in his heart - Satan has charged him with unbelief (FW). These legal charges (FW), have resulted in demonic entities entering his body causing fibromyalgia and brain fog (FW) thereby making things real tough at his job.

Because his body is aging normally, he can't see as well - but refuses (FW) to wear glasses. Jimmy can't see an order placed at the warehouse he works in, so Satan pokes at his anger and frustration (FW), causing Jimmy to lash out (FW) at his boss and get fired. Jimmy storms off from work (FW) and slams (FW) the car door - on his hand. In much pain, Jimmy decides to go to a bar and drink a few beers to feel better (FW). On the way home, driving drunk (FW) - he kills a 7 year-old in another vehicle.

How much of this is God responsible for??? **ZERO**.

How much could God have prevented??? **ZERO**.

As you can see, free will is such a large component of what comes to harm us. But when bad things do happen that are out of His control and that have snuck through our prayer net, we are called to persevere in **BELIEF (rest)**!

This might not sound like good news, but it is!! We don't wrestle with flesh and blood. This shapes our character, brings hope, leads us into spiritual maturity, shows us that we are who He says we are, reinforces our understanding of true spiritual authority, and grows us in the spirit realm. (Romans 5:1, 8:28; James 1:4, 1 Peter 1:7; Mark 16:17-20)

No, not all things are good, but The Lord is still good in all things. And all things will work out for our good, spiritually so that we can be mature and complete, lacking nothing in the spirit realm (James 1:4, Romans 8:28).

If you fully understood everything about God, your life, your troubles, your frustrations, and your future ... you would have no need to surrender. In fact, if you had *full* understanding your surrender would come from your own human understanding, and not His understanding.

You'd be your own God.

LEAVING THE 99

Surrender itself would be essentially faithless and lacking the spirit realm "faith currency" required to bring forth what you had thought you understood to be coming. Without a precious childlike surrender, God is just unable to be fully sovereign over our lives. We must live from this surrender to *make* Him Lord. He opposes the proud, even when they are His own kids.

Worse, without a genuine surrendered trust you won't be mature enough or even be in the right position to receive your full spiritual inheritance and the riches of Christ.

The sovereignty of The Lord in our lives as the *supreme power and authority*, will be directly proportional to our own level of surrender (rest). Yes, we get ourselves out of the way, so He can have His way! As sons and daughters, we have given up our right to fully understand! You died!

Friends, in that place of surrender and rest your voice is super powerful. Let me explain ...

I've done school traffic duty for 25 plus years, and among many things, I've learned that handicapped parking spots are meant for those with special blue placards. Yep, those attractive, well marked spots close to the front have been legally set aside for those who need them.

Yet, if I don't personally stand there and actively enforce what's been legally declared - anyone and everyone will park there. I've seen it happen right in front of the school a zillion times. And. Same with the cross.

God has declared us whole - spirit, soul, and body. Paid for in full. Stamped done! But, with our own tongues, we must enforce the legal decree at the cross - otherwise sickness, disease, demonic, and all things that have no legal right -

Alan Caplin

will park themselves in your body. For all things evil, you are an attractive parking spot because *you* are holy ground. Whatever *you* don't actively enforce with your own lips, will become trespassed.

After The Lord clearly speaks through Isaiah in chapter 53 about the provision of the cross, The Lord tells us that there is one who comes to destroy but ...

"no weapon that is fashioned against you shall succeed, and you shall refute every tongue that rises against you in judgment. This is the heritage of the servants of the LORD and their vindication from me, declares the LORD." Isaiah 54:17

From our own address seated in heaven, we ourselves must refute that lying tongue of evil! Not our prayer partner, not a friend, not a spouse, not a pastor, not an intercessor. These great prayer people will bring us peace, hope, help, relief, and provision for sure ... yet they literally are holding *you* up in prayer until *you* can stand on your own and refute the charges of darkness!

The Lord is **constantly** sending us healing through the oil of His own Spirit, but we *restrict* that oil flow by allowing demonic in through a door that Jesus shut 2,000 years ago.

Imagine a giant green garden hose flowing with healing oil – that has several kinks within it! The flow slows! Demonic brings the kinks. But we unkink that hose with repentance for our persistent unbelief. Yes, when the lips profess faith but the actions of the heart are contrary – this is where the devil is given time and space to bring charges of unbelief (James 2:12; 2 Timothy 2:19; Hebrews 2:1-3).

LEAVING THE 99

As an example of charges, Paul had been jailed and put on trial by the authorities ... and he was deserted by his own friends! These were followers of Jesus who boldly spoke of loving The Lord and were moving in great power – but in fear they "chickened out" of coming to stand with Paul.

"At my first defense no one came to stand by me, but all deserted me. May it not be charged against them!" 2 Timothy 4:16

Paul was praying that demonic charges wouldn't be able to take root in his friends from fear and disobedience!

When charges of unbelief come, we simply repent and point to our innocence in Jesus! Point to the blood. Point to the work of the cross. Point to who He is. Point to the empty tomb. And, tell the devil to flee!

"But he gives more grace. Therefore it says, "God opposes the proud but gives grace to the humble." Submit yourselves therefore to God. Resist the devil, and he will flee from you." James 4:6-7

In our pride The Lord opposes us, but in our humility and turning to Him ... grace and goodness freely flows. Many want to say "resist the devil and he will flee" but notice that we must **_first_** submit or surrender to God. Without this full surrender, we simply don't have the proper authority to tell the devil to flee from us!

Friends, we must guard our soul (heart and mind) for this is exactly how the devil enters to bring sickness!

"Beloved, I pray that all may go well with you and that you may be in good health, as it goes well with your soul." 3 John 2

Alan Caplin

It's like this, has anyone ever sold a house and then tried to throw in all the old furniture into the deal? You know, you toss in the old, junky furniture because you can make a few bucks or at very least you can save the hassle of hauling it away. Well. If you don't want that junky stuff, what makes us think the new owner wants it??

Upon belief, you made The Lord as The Sovereign of your own heart. Marked upon your heart with his own seal (2 Cor 1:22), you have been made His forever. Jesus now has sole ownership rights to all within the heart – and He is moving in to redecorate.

He made your heart His own - and He owns **ALL** the old furniture.

- Hurts
- Bruises
- Loss
- Grief
- Trauma
- Deep emotions
- Painful memories

The Lord desires to toss all that junky old furniture (ways of believing, thinking and emoting) into the fiery furnace. Yet. Some who gave the furniture away - weren't really ready to let it go to the new owner.

Folks, give Jesus sovereignty, let Him redecorate the rooms and spaces of your heart. For when The Lord decorates that room ... the demonic realm flees and takes *their* decorations with them!

LEAVING THE 99

Growing into Maturity

God loves you just because.

No strings.
No conditions.
No long forms to fill out.
No term contracts.
No expiration date.
No bait and switch.
No point deduction for misspelling and grammar.

He simply loves you because of who **HE** is! Friends, Jesus loved you *first* (1 John 4:19)! Please don't skip over this Truth, Jesus doesn't love us *back* because we love Him ... no, The Lord loved us first! And, from that place of being loved, that love compels us towards both Him and others.

NO-THING can **EVER** separate you from that perfect love - not your worst day, darkest fear, biggest secret, or deepest sin (Romans 8:38-39). But, Jesus also loves you *too* much to keep you the way He found you. Yes, we must mature as believers, otherwise we will never walk into true riches here in the earth. We will one day go to heaven, see Jesus and all the saints, and be like, "Man, I could have done that?????"

Friends, it's impossible to be clothed with "layers of new" when we are still clothed with the clunky, obsolete, and awkward layers of the old. New wine will always burst when clothed in the layers of old. Why? The old lacks the proper elasticity to handle the rigors and power of the new.

This is why God is working on your heart.

Alan Caplin

This is why God is pruning your identity.

This is why God is ripping out weeds from within you.

This is why God is stretching your inner capacity.

This is why God is making you feel uncomfortable.

Jesus wants to pour His new wine (The Holy Spirit) through you, that which your current ways of living and identifying cannot support. You'd be greatly crushed under the weight of responsibility! The Lord is reshaping and expanding the character of His own people, for the benefit of kingdom.

Folks, that *sack* of new wine is your *new* heart in Christ. Truly, without the heart taking on His character, the heart can't sustain the power of the Holy Spirit running through it! We must surrender the fullness of our hearts and clothe ourselves with Christ.

"Whoever believes in me, as the Scripture has said, 'Out of his heart will flow rivers of living water.'" John 7:38

From our hearts, the refined heart that has been grown into the pure reflection of Christ, the Holy Spirit will flow rivers of living water. Jesus, who dwells within your heart by faith (Ephesians 3:17) wants to pour His Spirit out through you!

Yet, over the years I've heard people say they find the term "Christ in you" as odd, and just can't find ways to relate to it. And that's ok, we are where we are. Here is the verse:

"To them God chose to make known how great among the Gentiles are the riches of the glory of this mystery, which is Christ in you, the hope of glory. Him we proclaim, warning

LEAVING THE 99

everyone and teaching everyone with all wisdom, that we may present everyone mature in Christ."Colossians 1:27-28

Verse 27: Christ in you. Verse 28: maturity.

Until you realize Christ dwells in you, you can't move into this spiritual maturity. To deny the spirit of Christ dwelling *within* you, is to deny absolutely everything that you are purposed to be. And once we realize the power of that spirit within, who can resist seeking and maturing into everything that God is and holds for us!

Many of us have received strong prophetic words about the plans The Lord has for us, but we struggle to see these plans manifest. We question if we are hearing right and wonder if those who spoke into us are legitimate carriers of His Glory. Yet, before God breaks a single promise to you, He'd have to first break His own covenant with the appointed arrivals of both day and night.

"The word of the Lord came to Jeremiah: "Thus says the Lord: If you can break my covenant with the day and my covenant with the night, so that day and night will not come at their appointed time, then also my covenant with David my servant may be broken, so that he shall not have a son to reign on his throne, and my covenant with the Levitical priests my ministers." Jeremiah 33:19-21

As my friend Grant Fraley says, "The work of The Lord is finished and fully provided for ... but it's not an *automatic* work." We in fact break His given promises by not actively participating in those released promises. Prophetic words are seeds that must be watered and nurtured.

The second a legitimate prophetic word is given, the devil is going to try to steal, kill, and destroy that word (seed). This

Alan Caplin

is why we must partner with that word, in *faith*. Truly, the picture on the outside of the package of seeds is what that seed is intended to look like at full maturity. Without us nourishing the seed, the seed cannot mature to full bloom.

The seed is the intention of the heart of the **One** who seeded the promise to you! That new seed (word) must be partnered with. We must feed that seed with our obedience, patience, prayer, preparation, perseverance, undivided attention, and our faith/belief.

It's His job to grow us and our character (soul) by the spirit, but it's our job to participate. Paul says in Romans 11 that the believing gentiles have been grafted into ... an olive tree. These are very slow, steady growing fruit bearing trees that are deeply representative of the land of Israel.

The roots/tree trunk are Jesus. The branches are *you*. The olives coming off your branches are the fruit of Jesus.

As a healthy branch, you are merely a conduit to the fruit being produced. You don't grow the fruit, Jesus does! All *you* do is draw life and nutrients from the tree trunk. That fruit, the olive, the fruit of righteousness is your character (Philippians 1:11).

Yes, as a work of the Spirit, our soul transforms into the very character of Jesus (2 Corinthians 3:18-19; Romans 8:29). But, how does the fruit (olive, character) growing from the tree of His Righteousness get converted into the flowing oil of Holy Spirit power?

Olives must be **PRESSED** to give up their oil!

Within your character, as you decrease and come to a place of full surrender and rest ... the anointing oil increases!! As

LEAVING THE 99

you rely less and less on you, and more and more on Jesus ... His oil flows from deep within you (2 Cor 4:7-12).

You died. You don't belong to you. By grace, all you need to expand the kingdom is freely yours. Jesus tells us, *"Fear not, little flock, for it is your Father's good pleasure to give you the kingdom." Luke 12:32*

Folks, after Jesus was placed in the tomb, the 11 remaining disciples hid in a locked room from the angry Jewish elite. They thought with Jesus they were now going to overthrow Rome - instead Jesus was dead and they saw no hope.

All of a sudden Jesus shows up and breathes the Holy Spirit and fresh life into them. Yes, the exact same life that God breathed into Adam. Jesus gave them the Holy Spirit *within*, a fresh peace, and new strength - more than enough to leave that room and face the angry mob.

So, if pressing and crushing brings the oil, don't be shocked if God changes you *before* the circumstance. Jesus did not change the angry mob, instead He changed His friends who had some kingdom work to do. In fact, I'm not so sure the angry mobs and threat of persecution ever changed as 10 of the 11 disciples died as martyrs (and they tried and failed to kill John in boiling oil).

I'm not saying your circumstances won't ever change, that's simply ludicrous. But The Lord wants you to persevere and keep going because perseverance brings kingdom hope and character. Perseverance brings maturity and makes sure we don't lack anything spiritually (Romans 5:3; James 1:4).

After we face trial and difficulty – Jesus promises to restore us and to make us firm (1 Peter 5:10). But while we do wait, maybe The Lord is waiting on us ....

Alan Caplin

Old attitudes must die.
Old mindsets must go.
Old habits must yield.
Old ways of self must bow.
Old thinking patterns must cease.

Again. Why? Freedom!!! To be fully free of self and world, we must know from the inside out that we are free. And that begins and ends in the spirit realm.

Many in the false grace and anti-religion circles get mad at me when I suggest that God wants us to grow. That God desires more. That God desires healthy change within us.

Yes, The Lord did away with the eternal consequences of our sin (Hebrews 9:26-28), but God isn't blind and He still sees us! Yes, all of ourselves, even the parts of us that are overgrown and need to be cut away.

We have been perfected in terms of sin (Hebrews 10:14), but not in terms of our "Christ like" moral character. Why else would Paul begin to suggest that suffering produces a heart shaped character that reflects heaven (Romans 5:3)?

The Lord has more for us, in us. Yes. Maybe, just maybe some storms simply won't calm until *we* are calm and at rest *in* the storm. Friends, when Jesus worries, we get to worry ... and Jesus never worries in a storm!

In writing to the Ephesians in Asia Minor, who had been besieged with the most demonic and evil obstacles to have ever been encountered back in that day, Paul implores the Ephesians to leave their infantile ways behind in order to become mature.

LEAVING THE 99

Speaking with truth in love, Paul implored them and us to maturity as the Body of Christ, in order to be in tune with the authority of the head of the body (Ephesians 4:14-16).

Maturity. It must happen for us to walk into our call and purpose. We simply can't be fully effective without it.

Loving others like Jesus isn't a high water mark we can't reach, it's flat out who we are in Christ. We are called to much greater works, which **must** include healing and the miraculous in order to in fact **BE** greater (John 14:12)!

Yet. When it comes to healing, false grace people say:

That was for the disciples. Or.
That was just for the 72. Or.
That ended with the temple fall. Or.
That died with the apostles. Or.
That only Jesus Himself can heal. Or.
Those verses aren't in the original text. Or.
That was only until the Bible was printed.

Or, maybe we don't **believe the gospel** (Mark 1:15). Love heals, fear cowers! The grace of God without faith working through **love** (Galatians 5:6) is nothing but noise. More so, both grace and love without healing, miracles, and displays of His own Glory, is a powerless and empty gospel.

I am about to make my **boldest** theological statement ever! Our inheritance is in Christ, right. And. The riches of Christ dwell within us, right (Ephesians 1:18; 2:7; 3:8).

Does an immature child receive their *full* inheritance? Of course not! They must first grow into a place of maturity.

Alan Caplin

That child might own 100% of everything, but have very little access to the vastness of his own wealth. The young child only has the use of a portion of what's rightfully his.

Until the kid grows up into adulthood, they don't get the whole kit and kaboodle. Why? The immature child simply isn't ready for the responsibilities of wealth.

- That's why we need to mature.
- That's why we need to grow up in Christ.
- That's why we are to feast on the meat of doing.

The gifts of Christ and the Holy Spirit are for the unification and building up of the church. Until we mature in both faith and love, we are settling for only a portion of what's ours.

"I mean that the heir, as long as he is a child, is no different from a slave, though he is the owner of everything, but he is under guardians and managers until the date set by his father." Galatians 4:1-2

You are no longer a small child, you are to become a mature son or daughter. The same way that the prodigal son had the legal right to his inheritance from the moment he asked, we too have a right to our inheritance (the riches in Christ) here and ***now***! You are a co-heir! You manage your own estate!! You aren't under the rule of a trustee. In a place of maturity, we have the right to our inheritance, ***here and now***!

Friends, it's time for the "Body of Christ" to mature. And, when it comes to maturity of the soul ... this verse has been badly misunderstood by the church:

"But no one can enter a strong man's (ischyros) house and plunder his goods, unless he first binds the strong man. Then indeed he may plunder his house." Mark 3:27

LEAVING THE 99

From the Blue Letter Bible Greek Translation App:
ischyros - of living beings: of one who has strength of soul to sustain the attacks of Satan, being strong and therefore exhibiting many excellences.

You as the believer, **YOU** are the ***strongman***! Nope, it's not the devil being bound, it's the devil binding the *soul* of the believer! A house divided against itself cannot stand (Mark 3:25). You are His house. You are His temple. You are the place He dwells.

Your soul is run by two engines: the heart and mind. Both think, both have conscious and subconscious thoughts. The double minded (or double souled) are bound by lies, doubts, fear, anxiety, opinions of others, hurtful memories, lusts of the world, false theology, and crooked thoughts as they are divided against themselves.

I've said this many times, when the mind and heart are at war. When the lips profess faith in Christ and yet the heart is distant and acting apart from belief - we as a living being are divided and we grant evil access through our own soul.

Double mindedness allows the devil to plunder your house.

- Giftings
- Spiritual Inheritances
- Relationships
- Opportunities
- Marriages, Families
- Purpose, Call
- Physical and Mental Health, Peace

Squandered, delayed, and stolen because we've been bound by our unbelief. You and your soul have been designed to withstand the attacks of Satan - because you know who you are and who you indeed belong to. In Christ, *you* my friend are the strongman!

My dear friend Chris Barhorst got me thinking even deeper about our maturity in Christ ... I'm now truly convinced that from this maturity we are called to "Hulk Smash" evil and the works of darkness. In fact, I'm also convinced that *not* being angry at the works of evil *is* a sin.

What's the secret to the Hulk's power? He's always angry!

As Chris points out: "Be angry" is present tense (always, here, now), passive voice (received from The Lord), and imperative (a command). Literally, this means that we are commanded by God to *constantly* receive *His* own anger towards sickness and evil. Not towards people, but towards that which keeps people both captive and imprisoned.

We are to speak truth in love, to bring others into maturity, and we are to push back against what evil has corrupted. We give the devil no opportunity to harass, and we refuse to let the sun set on this Holy anger for this righteous anger is the right response to that which demonic binds and holds back.

Hate sickness, disease, and works of evil. Love people.

"Therefore, having put away falsehood, let each one of you speak the truth with his neighbor, for we are members one of another. Be angry and do not sin; do not let the sun go down on your anger, and give no opportunity to the devil."
Ephesians 4:25-27

You died! You belong to another! It's time for the "Body of Christ" to mature and walk in the treasure of heaven ... the redemption, restoration, and righteousness of The Lord.

LEAVING THE 99

Seeking His Righteousness

Religion desires our works, and The Holy Spirit desires our faith. These are 2 drastically different methods of producing fruit from our righteousness (right standing) in Christ.

This is where many stand up and say, "But faith apart from works is dead!" Faith apart from works is absolutely dead ... because works of The Spirit flow from faith. Works do *not* produce faith, rather faith produces works!! The author of Hebrews tells us that the most elementary Christian doctrine urges us to repent **towards** God ... and turn **away** from *dead* works not born of faith (James 2:14-26; Hebrews 6:1).

Works of the flesh driven by the flesh, will always produce burn out and insecurity. Whereas, works of the Spirit born from faith and intimacy with The Lord will produce peace, joy, satisfaction, contentment, hunger for more of Him, and an ever-increasing strength to do these works of faith. The flesh brings death, but the Spirit brings life and peace!

"It is the Spirit who gives life; the flesh is no help at all."
John 6:63

Religion keeps us on a hamster wheel of performance, self-evaluation, and self-supply ... whereas the Holy Spirit wants to be our *full* supply in *all* things born of faith. Yes, religion forces us to work to "try" and be accepted by God ... when Jesus has already accepted us as brothers and sisters. Like the Prodigal Son's older brother - religion makes us **work** for the love of God that we *already* have! Our works will never be enough, when love from God is more than enough!

Alan Caplin

Friends, the righteous live by faith ... **not** by works! Truly, our faith works (Romans 1:17)!

I will keep saying it, **you died**! It was a single event that took place 2,000 years ago at the cross. Dead men have no need ... dead men **resting in peace** have full supply!

Yet religion will keep telling us to "die to self" or to "die daily" which in itself is an arduous process of self-works. Friends, Paul didn't crucify his flesh daily ... rather Paul faced death daily! We do not crucify the flesh, the flesh was *already* crucified! We simply have to *believe* it!

"I have been crucified with Christ. It is no longer I who live, but Christ who lives in me. And the life I now live in the flesh I live by faith in the Son of God, who loved me and gave himself for me." Galatians 2:20

When it comes to our righteousness or "right standing" in Christ - **legalism** and **false gracism** have opposite views. Legalists will create works to maintain right standing and gracists will minimize works declaring that we are already righteous or in right standing.

Well, both of these *extreme* positions are right ... to *some* degree. Let's dig into this a bit.

We must first start with understanding that we are a triune being consisting of *spirit, soul, and body* (1 Thessalonians 5:23). Secondly, we must lay out the definition of biblical terms. Without *proper* definitions, we will arrive at very inaccurate conclusions.

Righteousness for all practicality simply means being "in right standing" before The Lord. This right standing has 2 components: *justification* and *sanctification* (or holiness).

LEAVING THE 99

Justification is a term that means being made legally "just" before God. It's a legal way of saying you have been made "just" as if you had never sinned. This term refers to our *human spirit* (Proverbs 20:27) becoming **fused** with The Holy Spirit and our being *made alive* in Him (Colossians 2:13; Ephesians 2:5; 1 Corinthians 6:17). The spirit within us becomes justified and made perfect, just like Jesus!

Sanctification *(or holiness)* is the moral and relational component of our righteousness. This is our maturing identity in Christ and a constant work of the Holy Spirit within the believer *after* justification!

Sanctification is the transformation of the *soul* and our ever-increasing reflection of the image (soul) of Jesus (Romans 8:29; 1 Corinthians 1:18; 2 Corinthians 3:18). Although this can be seen as a type of process, more accurately, we are simply realizing more and more what is *already* true of us by The Spirit. The soul is catching up to where you already are in the spirit realm!

Sanctification is the same term as **holiness** – a maturation of the soul as one transforms into the image (or soul) of Christ. These two terms are often used interchangeably depending on the bible translation being used.

Glorification is of the flesh or *body*. Your body will fade away as your spirit lives on, but one day you will receive a new body made from His glory (1 Corinthians 15:35-58)!

Super simple! Your *spirit* is saved, your *soul* is being saved, and your *body* will one day be saved.

Jesus answered him, "Let it be so now, for thus it is fitting for us to fulfill all righteousness." Matthew 3:13-15

Alan Caplin

Jesus came to fulfill **all** righteousness – for both the spirit and the soul. This righteousness consists of two types:

1. **Imputed Righteousness**: This is simply *received* through belief. This is the eternal born again spirit.

2. **Imparted Righteousness:** This is *pursued* and is the transformation of the soul.

False gracism will say we are already righteous and don't need to have works attached to our faith. It's already been done. This is true to some degree as reflected *by the Spirit* and imputed righteousness. Your spirit is forever!

Legalists will say we need to do works to maintain our right standing with God and that we must be *doing*! This is also true to some degree with imparted righteousness ... as we *pursue* The Lord, the soul is transforming into the image (soul) of Jesus. However, this is a work of the Spirit *within* us and *not* a work of the flesh (2 Corinthians 3:18).

Imputed righteousness is received by grace through faith. *By the Spirit*, you have been made completely righteous because Jesus *IS* our righteousness! You have been made eternally righteous because Jesus is righteous and perfect. You are in right standing with The Father, because Jesus is in right standing with The Father! 24/7/365! No matter how hard you ever fall, Jesus is *still* righteous and holy! So, your righteousness isn't based on your own measured "goodness" or "badness" ... it is based on Him!

"Therefore, we are ambassadors for Christ, God making his appeal through us. We implore you on behalf of Christ, be reconciled to God. For our sake he made him to be sin who knew no sin, so that in him we might become the righteousness of God." 2 Corinthians 5:20-21

LEAVING THE 99

And because of him you are in Christ Jesus, who became to us wisdom from God, <u>righteousness</u> and sanctification and redemption, so that, as it is written, "Let the one who boasts, boast in the Lord." 1 Corinthians 1:30-31

Imparted righteousness is received over time! This is a hot pursuit! The only way for the soul to **transform** deeper and deeper into His image (soul) is by seeking after The Lord and His ways. This eternal life that begins here, now on this side of heaven ... must be taken hold of!

"But as for you, O man of God, flee these things. <u>Pursue righteousness</u>, godliness, faith, love, steadfastness, gentleness. Fight the good fight of the faith. <u>Take hold</u> of the eternal life to which you were called and about which you made the good confession in the presence of many witnesses." 1 Timothy 6:11-12

"So flee youthful passions and <u>pursue righteousness</u>, faith, love, and peace, along with those who call on the Lord from a pure heart." 2 Timothy 2:22

"But <u>seek</u> first the kingdom of God and his <u>righteousness</u> and all these things will be added to you." Matthew 6:33

With a little help from my friend Chris Barhorst, this below is one of my favorite revelations of scripture ... it might be the most powerful thing I could ever say or teach! It's one of those verses that we have taken for granted that we think we know what it says ...

"And we all, with unveiled face, beholding the glory of the Lord, are being transformed into the same image from one degree of glory to another. For this comes from the Lord who is the Spirit." 2 Corinthians 3:18

Alan Caplin

Tradition says that we go from glory to glory (from victory to victory) and we are changed along the way. Yes, that's true ... but that's not what *this* says!

In verses 3:1-17 Paul is talking about the veil that covers the face (and heart) of unbelievers, the freedom the Holy Spirit gives us, and the glory of Old Covenant vs. the surpassing glory of the New Covenant. Check this ... he then referring to these covenants goes on in verse 18 to say *"beholding the glory of the Lord (katoptrizo)"* we are being transformed.

Katoptrizo in the Greek (Blue Letter Bible App) means beholding as in a mirror!!! Paul is saying that when we believe, we look into a mirror and *SEE* the **GLORY OF THE NEW COVENANT!**

Jesus *is* the covenant (Isaiah 42:6; 49:8). So, when we look in the mirror of the New Covenant, we **SEE JESUS!** More importantly, we are being transformed into the *same* image that's *IN* the mirror ... Jesus!

Yes, by the Spirit (*justification, imputed*), when The Father looks at us, He sees Jesus! And by the soul (*sanctification, imparted*), we are *becoming* exactly like Jesus! Folks, Paul is not talking about victory to victory. Paul is saying that as we gaze into the mirror and glory of the new covenant - we are becoming transformed into the same **EXACT** character and image of Jesus! We are literally, *by pursuit*, becoming the One The Father sees in the mirror, Jesus!

Yes! As we continually gaze in that mirror of Truth our soul is being transformed to catch up to what is already true of us by the Spirit! Truly, when our human spirit and soul are in alignment with each other *and* with the Spirit of The Lord ... the devil has a huge problem on his hands!!

LEAVING THE 99

The Pharisees of old and The Pharisees of our modern-day religion have fallen into the same trap ... *self-righteousness*! A reliance on self, and not The Lord. Both work hard for love and approval, and attempt to make themselves right with The Lord.

Yet, in both the Old and New Testaments, our righteousness has **always** been by faith, **not** by works!!

"Behold, his soul is puffed up; it is not upright within him, but the righteous shall live by his faith." Habakkuk 2:4

For in it the righteousness of God is revealed from faith for faith, as it is written, "The righteous shall live by faith" Romans 1:17

Yes, the Israelites had been trying to obtain righteousness **through** the law as a work when the law was meant to be a way of teaching them how to live righteously with The Lord and others. Remember, when The Israelites had left Egypt, they were a pagan nation. They had no idea how to treat people, how to live with others, and how to relate to The Lord. The law was to be a guardian or school teacher until the Messiah would come (Galatians 3:24).

Most believers don't realize that the Israelites were to be **trained by the law to learn about faith righteousness, not to _make_ them righteous!** The works of the law were to be done by Israel in faith! These legalized works were to be done as **_acts of faith_** in the **_coming_** Messiah! But, Israel made the works of the law a measure of performance for being made right before The Lord!

"We ourselves are Jews by birth and not Gentile sinners; yet we know that a person is not justified by works of the law but through faith in Jesus Christ, so we also have

Alan Caplin

believed in Christ Jesus, in order to be justified by faith in Christ and not by works of the law, because by works of the law no one will be justified. I do not nullify the grace of God, for if righteousness were through the law, then Christ died for no purpose." Galatians 2:15-16, 21

By the works of the law, **no one** was justified!!!! If one could obtain righteousness through the works of the law, then there would have been no need for Jesus to die on the cross!!

"What shall we say, then? That Gentiles who did not pursue righteousness have attained it, that is, a righteousness that is by faith; but that Israel who pursued a law that would lead to righteousness did not succeed in reaching that law. Why? Because they did not pursue it by faith, but as if it were based on works." Romans 9:30-32

The Israelites did not pursue the law in faith, they did the law as a performance based work! Israel did the works of the law to be *made* righteous, but not by *faith* in the One they were "working" with!!!

Yes, our modern legalism is the same exact destructive formula Israel perished under! Mankind <u>always</u> has and <u>always</u> will be saved by His own goodness through faith! Eternal salvation will never be about our works, for then man will want to boast!

For by grace you have been saved through faith. And this is not your own doing; it is the gift of God, not a result of works, so that no one may boast. Ephesians 2:8-9

Legalism and religion have adopted the same work based mentality as Israel, but false gracism often proclaims that we don't need to mature because Christ is in us! I have had many tell me that we can't get any more mature (or

LEAVING THE 99

more sanctified/holy) because the work of The Lord was done and finished at the cross.

Then why does Paul say that some of the *unsaved* are holy?

So, if the unsaved can be set apart (or made holy) for The Lord and not have Christ in them - then how much more do the saved need to grow and mature into their holiness?

"For the unbelieving husband is made holy because of his wife, and the unbelieving wife is made holy because of her husband. Otherwise your children would be unclean, but as it is, they are holy." 1 Corinthians 7:14

It's simple really, but *false grace* teaching has a terrible misunderstanding of what holiness really is.

Saying you are a little bit holy, is the same thing as saying you are a little bit or 25% pregnant. You don't get more and more pregnant as you carry the baby ... the baby just comes to full term. The moment you receive Jesus you have become set apart or holy! You don't get more set apart, you move deeper into that place of being set aside for The Lord's use.

The same way a tiny baby girl just can't become any more "personier" - you simply can't become holier! A baby girl is a **PERSON** and matures into adulthood ... but always remains a person! Same thing with our holiness, we grow deeper! By The Lord, you are as set apart as you ever will be! But your moral character (soul) grows and transforms as you move deeper **IN** your holiness.

This is exactly why the unsaved spouse is holy. You can set a table, chair, guitar, or computer aside as being holy to The Lord ... yet it doesn't mean the "thing" or "object" is _**living**_! If the unbelieving spouse doesn't ever come to believe in Jesus as Lord, they remain set apart or holy ... but haven't been _**made alive**_ by The Spirit! Sadly, they are still an unregenerate, non-living spirit.

We have been set apart by The Spirit, _**once**_ for all!

"And by that will we have been sanctified through the offering of the body of Jesus Christ once for all."
Hebrews 10:10

Yet, those set apart are _**being**_ sanctified!

"For by a single offering he has perfected for all time those who are being sanctified." _Hebrews 10:14_

We are eternally justified by The Spirit through our heart belief, yet our salvation (wholeness of spirit, soul, and body) is dependent upon what we confess as being true! Yes, what we confess from our lips is either His Truth or our own truth. This belief and confession of belief will always be a function of our sanctified maturity!

"For with the heart one believes and is justified, and with the mouth one confesses and is saved." _Romans 10:10_

Friends, until you are walking on water or converting water into wine - your soul must transform into His own image. Even then, there's still greater (John 14:12). Yet, unlike The Pharisees, we must fervently pursue and seek His Righteousness (Jesus) and go after our _**one thing**_.

_"But seek first the kingdom of God and his _Righteousness_ (Jesus), and _all_ these _things_ will be added to you."_
Matthew 6:3 (emphasis added by me for clarity)

LEAVING THE 99

Covenant Promises

For me, the epicenter of the gospel message comes out of **Romans 6:3** and the foundational Truth that *"You died!"* Every other theological construct must both begin and end with this Truth. Grasping this powerful concept of having been _permanently_ immersed into the death and life of Christ ... is critical to a healthy, fruitful, long lasting, and purpose filled walk with Jesus.

Once we grasp *"You died"* and that *you* don't provide for *you* – we must then firmly understand *covenant* and what that means for us.

"For you have died, and your life is hidden with Christ in God." Col 3:3

The words *"with"* and *"in"* are covenant language terms!! Literally, you died with Christ **and** you have been **hidden forever** inside the covenant with Jesus, and hidden in Jesus as He is then hidden in covenant with the Father! Friends, you have been tucked away in Christ as Jesus Himself has been tucked away inside the Father! There is no safer place than being fully dead to yourself, safely hidden away in the hands of Jesus ... Who is hidden away forever in the Father!

Covenant, for lack of better terms, is an agreement upon a set of terms or contract. Although there are many different types of covenants, this is an explicit arrangement between 2 separate parties.

There is no better biblical example of covenant than the Israelites dealing with Goliath and the Philistines. Goliath

Alan Caplin

had been violently taunting Israel for 40 days and nights, and Goliath shouts at Israel:

"If he is able to fight and kill me, we will become your subjects; but if I overcome him and kill him, you will become our subjects and serve us." 1 Samuel 17:9

Israel had chosen David, and the Philistines of course chose their massive Goliath. Each nation had agreed that David and Goliath would be the ***covenant representative*** for each people group. It was winner take **all**, for **all** the people! If your guy wins, then you win! If your guy loses, you lose! The people would get what their representative procured.

Yes, Jesus is our covenant representative! We get what He earned! We are victorious because He was victorious! The covenant representative did **not** pick and choose who got to share in the victory or loss. If you entered into covenant by accepting terms with the representative ... you were part of the treaty, end of story!

If we want to see how seriously The Lord views covenant, all we need to do is look at Israel and The Gibeonites. The Gibeonites had tricked Israel into a covenant of protection, and Israel was forced to honor this sacred covenant because otherwise the wrath of The Lord would fall on Israel!

"The whole assembly grumbled against the leaders, but all the leaders answered, "We have given them our oath by the LORD, the God of Israel, and we cannot touch them now. This is what we will do to them: We will let them live, so that God's wrath will not fall on us for breaking the oath we swore to them." Joshua 9:18-20

Even though Israel had been badly deceived, the covenant **had to stand** because of the integrity of The Lord. More

LEAVING THE 99

importantly, the Gibeonites had intentionally lied to Israel ... yet Israel herself suffered a 3 year famine because Saul had been persecuting the Gibeonites.

"While David was king there was a time without food for three years. David went to the Lord. The Lord said, "It is because of Saul and his house of blood, for he put the Gibeonites to death." 2 Samuel 21:21

I promise you, you have not tricked Jesus into being your covenant representative. If The Lord honored those who entered a covenant of protection through deception, how much **more** does He honor those who enter the covenant of eternal protection (salvation) through heartfelt belief.

"the righteousness of God through faith in Jesus Christ for all who believe." Romans 3:22

"For Christ is the end of the law for righteousness to everyone who believes." Romans 10:4

On the basis of the Mosaic covenant between The Lord and Israelites, for many years I had mistakenly thought the **New Covenant** was between The Lord and mankind. The Mosaic covenant was an "if-then" arrangement. If you do this, that happens. If you do that, this happens. As we all know, this covenant just didn't fare well for Israel. So, having been raised Jewish, I was like, "Surely I *can* mess this thing up!"

Yet, who were the 2 parties that ratified the **New Covenant**?

"If I am not doing the works of my Father, then do not believe me; but if I do them, even though you do not believe me, believe the works, that you may know and understand that the Father is in me and I am in the Father." John 10:37-38

Again, the word **"in"** is critical covenant language. Notice, *"the Father is in me and I am in the Father."* This covenant was ratified between the Father and the Son!

The Father and Son sit in covenant with *each other* - not for their benefit - but for the benefit of their own creation! Jesus *IS* the actual covenant (Isaiah 42:6; Isaiah 49:8) and this covenant was put into effect between these 2 separate parties (who do *not* change and *cannot* lie) <u>***before time began***</u> (Hebrews 4:3; Hebrews 6:18) *and* was ratified by both the blood and resurrection (Colossians 2:12-15).

Friends, you and I weren't there when the covenant was created and put into effect!! We weren't part of the *treaty* because The Lord knew that we'd surely mess this up!

For the Father to ever deny you or me, He'd have to *first* deny His covenant partner Jesus (2 Timothy 2:13)! Truly, no matter how bad things may seem at times - we have never left, made void, or ever broken the covenant with The Lord (yes - we can and do *fall away*, I will touch on that in the next chapter on eternal security).

The Father and Son are One. If you've seen Jesus, then you've seen the Father (Hebrews 1:3). And by the Spirit, *you* are One in Christ. If they've seen *you*, then they've seen Jesus (2 Corinthians 3:18).

To me, this is an amazing picture of our covenant: *And he said to them, "When I sent you out with no moneybag or knapsack or sandals, did you lack anything?" They said, "Nothing." Luke 22:35*

By faith, the disciples went out across Israel as the hands and feet of Jesus – yes, as The Body of Christ. And, they lacked absolutely <u>nothing</u>! In this <u>unconditional</u> covenant

LEAVING THE 99

with The Lord, as you *rest in peace (RIP)*, Jesus becomes your full supply!!

Adam and Eve fell, a covenant was needed to restore man to our rightful relationship with God. If not for *the* covenant of Jesus, there wouldn't **BE** a personal relationship! Truly, we only have access to the Father through Jesus.

You and I have far *more* than only a personal relationship with The Lord as a son or daughter ... we have a powerful "covenantal relationship" with The Lord where everything that He has is ours and all that we have is His!

We have an unconditional, covenantal, and deeply personal relationship with The Lord that provides much more than most imagine or understand along with personal intimacy with God (which was unobtainable prior to the blood and the cross).

Yes. We have and we are because of **WHO** He is.

- Everything He has we have.
- Everything He is, so are we.
- Everything Jesus did we can do.

Unlike fragile earthly relationships with your spouse, co-worker, pastor, neighbor, employer, friend, or dentist ... the relationship we have with The Lord *cannot* ever be broken!

Friends, we were **created and purposed with Jesus in this permanent covenant** ... always remember that the term *"in Christ"* is covenant language.

*"For we are his workmanship, created **in** Christ Jesus (covenant) for good works, which God prepared*

*beforehand, that we should walk in them." Ephesians 2:10 (**covenant** and emphasis added by me for clarity)*

Once we understand the basis of His covenant - our identity as co-heirs becomes quickened and we can't help but walk like Jesus walked. Both bold and fearless!

When I put my hands on someone to pray, I do so knowing by covenant God is going to show up. When trouble comes or needs become apparent, I can truly **rest in peace** because I know that I sit in this perfect covenant. Remember, you are only able to come before the Father ... in the name of Jesus. We have no access of our own. We only have access because of the covenant (Jesus).

Friends, once entered in through heart felt belief (Romans 10:10), we have an iron clad covenant with The Lord that we just can't mess up! This covenant gives us life here, now and forever in the intimate presence of God. Yes, the Father calls me son, **because** Jesus came **before** me.

My buddy Roger Armstrong once said to me, "The further you go with Jesus, the less you can bring with you." The truth of this statement rocked me! Insecurities, fears, ways of the world, and our self-reliance must be left behind for the full supply and riches of this covenant (or *legal will*).

"For where a will is involved, the death of the one who made it must be established. For a will takes effect only at death, since it is not in force as long as the one who made it is alive. Therefore not even the first covenant was inaugurated without blood." Hebrews 9:16-17

The word *covenant* in the Greek is *diatheke*. According to the **Blue Letter Bible Translation App**, the word *diatheke* means "the last disposition which one makes of his earthly

LEAVING THE 99

possessions after his death, a testament or will." My friends, think about this, Jesus had to die to leave you His riches! By His blood, Jesus has given us access to vast spiritual wealth!

Yes, Jesus included you in His *last will and testament*, and He has left you a vast fortune. All you have to do is believe that it's yours! *All you do is seek this treasure by faith!*

"And he said to them, "This is my blood of the covenant (diatheke), which is poured out for many." Mark 14:24 (emphasis and diatheke added for clarity)

Yes, the *new covenant* is actually a last will and testament that has been ratified by His own death and blood! So, the question you are now probably asking yourself is, "Why did Jesus do this for us, and why did Jesus leave *me* a fortune?"

Super simple answer ... because of the unconditional and everlasting covenant with Abraham!

When the covenant with Abram was cut by The Lord in Genesis 15, Abram wasn't involved in that treaty *either*! The Father and Jesus created this covenant together while Abram was fast asleep (Genesis 15:12). This agreement in *totality* rests upon The Lord and The Lord alone to bring to pass. All Abram had to do was *believe* The Lord that the spoken promise was true!

"Abram believed the LORD, and he credited it to him as righteousness." Genesis 15:6

So, *what* promise had Abram believed???

He took him outside and said, "Look up at the sky and count the stars—if indeed you can count them." Then he said to him, "So shall your offspring be." Genesis 15:5

Alan Caplin

Abram believed that The Lord would make a great nation from his own descended heir. This nation isn't Israel! This nation are those who believe in Jesus Christ (***the*** offspring), and those in covenant with Jesus are the directly descended offspring of Abram (Galatians 3:16; Galatians 3:29).

Track me here, The Lord has left us vast supernatural wealth to go get Abraham his promise of <u>descendants</u>!

Yes, Jesus has made you to be just like Himself to honor the promises made to Abraham! The Lord desires to make you supernaturally rich to go get the work of the kingdom done!

ALERT!!!!!!!! Knowing all that I have written so far in this book - please, please read this next long verse very slowly, and with great intent. You will never see the bible the same way again!!! This verse will surely amaze you, and you will see ***why*** you are here as a believer!!! You will now see ***why*** He has left you a great spiritual inheritance!

The Spirit of the Sovereign LORD is on me,
    because the LORD has anointed me
    to proclaim good news to the poor.
He has sent me to bind up the brokenhearted,
    to proclaim **<u>freedom for the captives</u>**
    and **<u>release from darkness for the prisoners</u>**,
² to proclaim the year of the LORD's favor
    and the day of vengeance of our God,
to comfort all who mourn,
³   and provide for those who grieve in Zion—
to bestow on them a crown of beauty
    instead of ashes,
the oil of joy
    instead of mourning,
and a garment of praise
    instead of a spirit of despair.

LEAVING THE 99

They will be called oaks of righteousness,
   a planting of the LORD
   for the **display of his splendor**.
⁴ **They** will rebuild the ancient ruins
   and restore the places long devastated;
they will renew the ruined cities
   that have been devastated for generations.
⁵ Strangers will shepherd your flocks;
   foreigners will work your fields and vineyards.
⁶ And **you** will be called **priests of the LORD**,
   you will be **named ministers of our God**.
You will feed on the wealth of nations,
   and in their riches **you** will boast.
⁷ Instead of your shame
   you will receive a **DOUBLE PORTION**,
and instead of disgrace
   you will **rejoice in your inheritance**.
And so **you** will inherit a **double portion** in your land,
   and everlasting joy will be **yours**.
⁸ "For I, the LORD, love justice;
   I hate robbery and wrongdoing.
In my faithfulness I will **reward my people**
   and *make an everlasting covenant with them*.
⁹ Their descendants will be known among the nations
   and their offspring among the peoples.
All who see them will acknowledge
   that they are a people the LORD has blessed."
¹⁰ I delight greatly in the LORD;
   my soul rejoices in my God.
For he has **clothed me with garments of salvation**
   and **arrayed me in a robe of his righteousness**,
as a bridegroom adorns his head like a priest,
   and as a **bride** adorns herself with her jewels.
¹¹ For as the soil makes the sprout come up
   and a garden causes seeds to grow,

Alan Caplin

so the **Sovereign LORD will make righteousness and praise spring up <u>before all nations</u>**.
Isaiah 61:1-11(emphasis added by me for clarity)

Verses 1-2 are obviously speaking of Jesus, and even Jesus quotes this verse in the temple right after returning from the desert (Luke 4:18). However, notice that Jesus Himself sets free the captives and lets the prisoners out of darkness.

Captives are there against their will, these are the oppressed. Prisoners are there because of their own poor choices. Jesus sets both these people groups free ... and these freed people ... become those who free others doing the work of Jesus! In this verse, the *"they"* and *"you"* ... are <u>**YOU**</u> the priests of The Lord, the bride of Christ!

Yes, the oppressed, burdened, frustrated, tired, stuck, and those who have been placed under the spiritual burden of "lock and key" ... will inherit the supernatural power of our Jesus and the role of making His righteousness spring up in the nations!!!

This is *why* we *<u>leave</u>* the 99!! Jesus wants to bless *you*, so *you* can bless Abraham! Yes, He wants you blessed to be a blessing! Yes, Jesus wants to supernaturally bless you with the *double portion anointing* to get much needed kingdom work done (verse 7)!

I will cover this double portion anointing in chapter 14. I promise, you will be amazed!!

"We are therefore Christ's ambassadors, as though God were making his appeal through us." 2 Corinthians 5:20

LEAVING THE 99

Eternal Security

A few months ago I stumbled upon a documentary about Mister Rogers' Neighborhood called ***"Won't You Be My Neighbor" (2018)***. Fred Rogers was an ordained minister and was a man of deep faith. Aside from many testimonies within this film, one just needs to look at the sheer fruit of his own television ministry to know about his faith.

Yet, as Fred Rogers took ill and neared the end of his life, he asked his wife if she thought he was a sheep or goat. I'd like to point out, that in the parable of the lost sheep (Luke 15:1-7), the sheep ***never*** became a goat!!

Despite persecution, protest, name calling, and hate ... Fred Rogers shaped the hearts of millions of children; spoke to our kids about difficult subjects like racism, wars, divorce, shame, assassination, rejection, sadness, and anger; infused identity into lost little ones; and everything he said, lived, and did was rooted and grounded in love (143).

Mister Rogers greatly shaped a broken generation, and this neighborhood ***now*** needs men and women to rise up like Fred Rogers. Still, Mister Rogers didn't even know if he was a sheep or goat! Seems as a minister he never learned his own identity in Christ, ***first***.

If this could happen to a man so in love with Jesus, and to one where massive lines and crowds formed just to see him ... then imagine how this can happen to those who don't "see" their personal influence within the lives of others.

Alan Caplin

This is why balanced teaching on our *identity* in Christ is so very important, and this is truly why understanding ancient covenant is so critical to grasp.

The false teaching of *legalism* and *gracism* are snares to our peace and fruit. One makes you work to be a sheep, and the other in great apathy denies there are even goats! Sadly, at least legalism builds kingdom and leaves a legacy of love in Christ. Yet still, Mister Rogers was not only a sheep, he was a giant of the faith.

If you have struggled with worrying about your salvation like Mister Rogers, I pray that you are being nourished by what I've been saying about our union or being made *alive* in The Lord and our covenant with Him.

This next concept may also help. Some verses get said over and over again, without checking out what the verse really, truly says. Grace people love this verse, and it's used all the time to say we don't need to receive correction from people. Or, our feelings shouldn't ever be hurt by being taken to the carpet for our attitudes or behavior.

"There is therefore now no condemnation for those who are in Christ Jesus." Romans 8:1

Romans 8:1 isn't talking about embarrassment, shame and guilt - it's speaking about eternal damnation. Paul is writing in chapter 7 about the law/sin, and the ensuing death and damnation that had resulted. Here, he transitions in chapter 8 about our life by the Spirit. Paul is talking about the truth that you as a believer now reside in the spirit realm and will *never* lose your salvation! You are forever, because you sit in an unbreakable covenant.

LEAVING THE 99

The word condemnation here is *katakrima*, and this word **(Blue Letter Bible App)** means damnatory sentence. Yes, eternal judgment! And, remember the phrase "in Christ" is covenant language.

So, technically this verse would better read: **"There is therefore now no death sentence for those who are in covenant with Christ Jesus." Romans 8:1**

If you are "in Christ" or in covenant with Christ, you will *never* be put to eternal shame (Isaiah 45:22-25).

I'd also like to add this thought about eternal security. We are quick to believe that if someone receives Jesus on their deathbed they become saved, but we are too equally quick to say that someone who receives Jesus as a teen and has a life filled with strife, abuse, hardship, struggle, rape, drugs, alcohol, addiction, fear, and pain would now **not** be saved because they have fallen back in faith.

So, one carries the spiritual football 2 yards to the goal line, and one must carry the ball from goal line to goal line?

Zero sense that makes! Our eternity isn't earned. Jesus did that. Anything less would be salvation based upon works, not by grace through faith (Ephesians 2:8). Truly, those given to Jesus by the Father - will 100% find their way home. Not one shall Jesus lose, simply because His name, promise, righteousness, and reputation depends upon it!

"And this is the will of him who sent me, that I shall lose none of all those he has given me, but raise them up at the last day." John 6:39

Alan Caplin

"Very truly I tell you, whoever hears my word and believes him who sent me has eternal life and will not be judged but has crossed over from death to life." John 5:24

The moment you believe, you have crossed over the goal line from death to life. The moment you believe, you will ***not*** be judged, because you have already been judged by covenant as innocent at the cross!

Friends, please remember! Righteousness is a gift of God by the grace of God (Romans 5:17; Ephesians 2:8-9) and yet, God's *gifts* and call may never be ***revoked*** (Romans 11:29). Your eternal salvation is a gift from God by His grace and by His own word ... The Lord *cannot* and will ***not*** revoke your free gift of life. The Lord's integrity depends on it!

I have written much across these last few chapters about our eternal security, but many will certainly still be confused by poor interpretations of scripture that you've been exposed to. So, I am going to spend some time covering 2 separate biblical areas: **sin** (*repentance*) and **falling away** (*book of Hebrews*). **Sin** and **falling away** are two areas that function together - but for many bring some confusion and difficulty.

Sin (Repentance):

There are only 2 possible sin payment plans. Either, pre-paid by Jesus in full at the cross or "pay as you go" with repentance and confession.

1. The way *legalists* deal with sin is to say that we must continually repent to keep ourselves clean.

2. The way *false gracists* deal with sin is to say all sin is put away and **all** are saved.

LEAVING THE 99

Friends, the truth is somewhere in the middle.

Yes, we repent (Hebrew: teshuva) - by turning towards Him from our own heart and inner most being. Yes, our heartfelt repentance from deep within is a very powerful weapon for breaking off demonic accusations/charges of our unbelief. Yes, repentance is a key to not falling prey to the schemes of the enemy. Yes, repentance brings our relationship with God back into alignment. Yes, repentance is a *lifestyle*!

Yes, confession flows *from* our repentance! Confession is where we turn to the Lord and say, "Yes, I have been doing or feeling XYZ, and I need help, I just can't fix this without You!" Confession brings inner and physical healing as this is often a necessary part of breakthrough (James 5:16).

But, ***ALL*** sin had been upon the flesh of Jesus, ***once***! Sin has been ***put away*** (Hebrews 9:25-28; Colossians 2:13-15).

"Christ, having been offered once to bear the sins of many, will appear a second time, not to deal with sin but to save those who are eagerly waiting for him." Hebrews 9:28

Sin had been dealt with once, and Jesus will one day return to bring salvation to those who wait ... not to deal with sin again! All sin has been dealt with *once* - by *one* offering - for yesterday, today, and tomorrow! Jesus doesn't jump on and off the cross each time we mess up. He entered heaven - once, for **all**. In fact, not only did Jesus pay the price for the sin of the world *once*, but He actually paid **DOUBLE**! Yes, Jesus even overpaid! (John 1:29; 1 John 2:2; Isaiah 40:2).

But. No, **not** all are saved! Upon **belief**, just like Abraham, the payment that Jesus made is credited back to **us** as His righteousness (Romans 4:20-25; Galatians 2:6).

No, saying sorry over and over doesn't cleanse us. The cross did that. Friend, no matter how hard you try, you can't open an account of sin against you that God has already closed!

- How else would you for sure know that you've been forgiven?

- How else would unconfessed sin be covered?

- How else could we pass away without saying sorry for things that we missed?

- How else could we die unexpectedly without full confession and get a pass to heaven?

Can we be disobedient - yes.
Can we destroy our lives - yes.
Can we harm people we care about - yes.
Can we grieve The Lord - yes.
Can we sabotage plans The Lord has for us - yes.
Can we give the devil a spiritual foothold – yes.
Can we invite evil into our bodies through the soul – yes.

New covenant sin is absolutely bad. It will destroy the plans of God in your life and it will wreak havoc on your *soul* and *body* ... but your *spirit* is eternal. Remember, salvation itself (wholeness) is a function of spirit, soul, and body.

Grace folks who preach that all sin is paid for, do a terrible disservice to the Body of Christ by not ***equally*** teaching you died, you were made alive *for* God, you no longer belong to yourself, ***AND*** that acts of ***unbelief*** flowing from within the ***heart*** will bring demonic entities (and discipline) into your own life (Hebrews 2:2-3; 2 Timothy 2:19; 2 Timothy 4:16; 1 Peter 4:17; Acts 5:3; Acts 8:21; Luke 22:31; Mark 7:6-8; 1 Corinthians 11:27-32; Hebrews 12:7-11; Psalm 89:34).

LEAVING THE 99

The only way to be free *from* sin is to be free *to* sin. You got it. If you don't have a choice, you aren't really free.

"For one who has died has been set free from sin."
Romans 6:7

I'd like to take a moment to address the *unpardonable sin*. First, let me tell you why the answer to this question is so very, very important. I've met many people who have had relatives commit suicide because they thought they were eternally damned for blasphemy of the Holy Spirit.

After casting out demons by the power of the Holy Spirit or the finger of God (Matthew 12:31-32), who here is Jesus speaking to? Who are these words applicable to? Yep, the Pharisees, **_unbelievers_** who had been rejecting the work of the Spirit through Jesus. The Pharisees had been calling the work of Jesus the work of the devil. So, you have to be an **UNBELIEVER** to commit this eternal sin.

It's **THE SIN** of unbelief! This is a rejection of salvation itself because it's a rejection of the Spirit's work from and through Jesus.

Rejection of eternal salvation is the only sin not upon His flesh, otherwise we'd *all* be saved. As previously written, there is no eternal condemnation or damnable sentence for those secure in covenant with Christ Jesus (Romans 8:1).

All of this stuff written about sin, to now define what sin is under the New Testament (covenant). It's unbelief, it's the *fruit* of unbelief! It's those attitudes and thoughts that are **not** of God, that flow **outward** from the **heart of man**!

The Lord has dealt with the eternal consequences of sin one time, but He is *always* dealing with our hearts! We are no longer separated from The Lord by *sin* (Hebrews 10:19-22), rather we are separated from Him in our own *unbelief* and *faulty believing*! Yes, sin has been dealt with once, but the thorns and thistles (weeds of unbelief) inside the heart will always need regular lawn care (Matthew 13:7)!

I'd like to further simplify the understanding of what new covenant sin truly is. To do that, these are the verses that clarify or define ***post-cross*** sin:

- Anything not done in faith is sin (Romans 14:23).

- The good that we know to do and yet do <u>*not*</u> do is sin (James 4:17).

- Any and all wrongdoing is sin. Therefore anything done *wrong* because we aren't believing *right* ... is sin (1 John 5:17).

- As written previously, <u>***be***</u> angry at the works of evil to push them back and do not sin (Ephesians 4:26).

Each one of these verses have something in common, that's <u>*unbelief*</u>. **Sin** is just that, it's the *iniquity* (both thoughts and attitudes) of the heart and the *transgressions* (actions) that flow from those places of deep <u>*unbelief*</u>. Essentially, it's all that flows from within that is born of self and the world, and not of The Lord. Unbelief (sin) won't necessarily *damn* you, but it will absolutely *destroy* you, here!

Having explained new covenant sin, I can now connect this deeper understanding to *falling away*, and more specifically to the book of Hebrews.

LEAVING THE 99

Falling Away (the Book of Hebrews):

Whenever I suggest eternal salvation isn't something to be earned, nor lost, nor maintained ... many like to use verses from the book of Hebrews to say that we can lose the free gift of salvation. Yes, if read out of context, I can see what they are saying – but verses must be taken into full context in order for *true* understanding.

The two main verses often used out of context are:
Hebrews 6:1-8
Hebrews 10:26-27

Before I get into these two verses, let me give you a little backdrop on the book of Hebrews. This book is written to Jewish "believers" who are leaving the faith and running right back to the temple system. Facing heavy persecution by the Jewish elite, these "believers" are leaving for the safety of their own culture. Yes, these Jewish "believers" are *falling away* from the faith and the author is writing a persuasive essay to help them better see the Truth of Jesus!

Remember back to what I was saying about sin, ***unbelief is sin.*** Sin is not just a list of really bad things (or actions) that we choose to do. The author doesn't list sins like adultery, coveting, murder, drunkenness, sexual immorality, idolatry, thieving, et cetera. The book of Hebrews is about one type of sin ... those who *fall away from an unbelieving heart*.

"Take care, brothers, lest there be in any of you an evil, unbelieving heart, leading you to fall away from the living God." Hebrews 3:12

The book is speaking about their own unbelief which failed them in the desert, which robbed them of His promises, and for *some*, which threatens to steal their hope of salvation.

Alan Caplin

When Hebrews 12:1 is read in the Greek *(Blue Letter Bible App)*, we clearly see this book is about **THE** sin, <u>unbelief</u>!! Friends, *the sin* is a failure to both believe and rest in Jesus as Lord (Hebrews chapters 3 and 4). The author is writing about the *condition of the heart* of those Jewish people who are leaving the faith.

*"Therefore, since we are surrounded by so great a cloud of witnesses, let us also lay aside every weight, and **(the)** sin which clings so closely"* Hebrews 12:1 (emphasis and "the" added by me for clarity).

If we want to say the author is telling these people they will now lose their salvation, then the author had to of been very badly confused because he also says, *"I will never leave nor forsake you."* Hebrews 13:5

Again, before I get into these two misused verses – I want to *briefly* remind everyone about the parable of the sower (Matthew 13:1-23). In this parable there are **four** heart types, and each type is a believer of some shape or form. The seed is the word of God and the soil is the heart of man.

Heart type **one** received the seed as it fell upon the heart, but it was quickly snatched away to steal their salvation. This seed **never took root** within the heart.

Heart type **two** received the seed, it fell upon soil that was receptive to a degree. But there was solid rocky ground just beneath the little bit of topsoil. The seed brought some life out from the heart ... for a short while. But then persecution came, destroying the growth from the heart, and the person **falls away** as there was **no root** within the heart.

Heart type **three** receives the seed, but the soil (or heart) is filled with weeds (thorns and thistles). The seed **does takes**

LEAVING THE 99

root, but the weeds choke out the growth of the seed. This soil (heart) produces a crop from the heart, but it is sickly, weak, and badly malnourished (I believe this is most of the church today).

Heart type **four**, receives the seed with a great joy and with understanding. The seed **takes root**, and the heart produces a healthy crop of 30, 60, 100.

Not all four heart types are saved. Heart types one and two have **no root**, and James tells us that we are saved by the rooted or implanted word (James 1:21). Yet, heart types of three and four **have a root**, and are saved.

The majority of the *intended* audience here are from heart type **TWO** ...

"yet he has no root in himself, but endures for a while, and when tribulation or persecution arises on account of the word, immediately he falls away." Matthew 13:21

Yes, this book is predominantly written to "believers" who aren't saved ... heart type **two** being persecuted and falling away. You simply can't lose what you never had!

So, we see there are four distinct and separate heart types that the seed or word of God falls upon. If the seed is the word of God, and it is sown, then that means every single book of the bible is written to **ALL** four heart types. No, not every verse in the bible is written to all the four types. Yes, we can learn and grow from each and every verse, but *no*, not every verse is speaking to the heart condition of every believer.

It's like this. If a school bus driver in frustration looks up in his mirror and says, "If you kids don't stop jumping up and down screaming I am going to turn this bus around!" Well, every kid on that bus is operating in different degrees of non-compliance. In fact, I'm sure some are even being well behaved. The statement is for the *whole* group, but not for each *individual* on the bus!

That's the book of Hebrews, it's written to the whole. It's written to people with different degrees of belief. Some are rooted (saved) and some aren't. As entire families left the faith together, each person had different degrees of faith in The Lord.

So, now let's tackle these two verses. Let's start with:

"For if we go on sinning deliberately after receiving the knowledge of the truth, there no longer remains a sacrifice for sins, but a fearful expectation of judgment, and a fury of fire that will consume the adversaries."
Hebrews 10:26-27

Remember, the bulk of this audience are heart types 1 and 2 ... and the book is about <u>the sin of unbelief</u> after hearing the word of God (seed). So, watch this ...

*"For if we go on **unbelieving** deliberately after receiving the knowledge of the truth, there no longer remains a sacrifice for sins, but a fearful expectation of judgment, and a fury of fire that will consume the adversaries."*
Hebrews 10:26-27 (sinning swapped with unbelieving and emphasis added by me).

For salvation to occur knowledge must become more than just information received, this knowledge must be **birthed** from within. This is where the rooting takes place. As you can see, this verse is about those who received knowledge

LEAVING THE 99

of truth, but weren't as *yet* saved by it. Not every believer is saved!!

Let's now tackle this verse:

"Therefore let us leave the elementary doctrine of Christ and go on to maturity, not laying again a foundation of repentance from dead works and of faith toward God, [2] and of instruction about washings, the laying on of hands, the resurrection of the dead, and eternal judgment. [3] And this we will do if God permits. [4] For it is impossible, in the case of those who have once been enlightened, who have tasted the heavenly gift, and have shared in the Holy Spirit, [5] and have tasted the goodness of the word of God and the powers of the age to come, [6] and then have fallen away, to restore them again to repentance, since they are crucifying once again the Son of God to their own harm and holding him up to contempt. [7] For land that has drunk the rain that often falls on it, and produces a crop useful to those for whose sake it is cultivated, receives a blessing from God. [8] But if it bears thorns and thistles, it is worthless and near to being cursed, and its end is to be burned." Hebrews 6:1-8

This verse is speaking to those who need to **LEAVE** the elementary teachings and **MOVE** to maturity. In fact, let's look at the verses immediately *preceding* Hebrews 6:1-8:

"About this we have much to say, and it is hard to explain, since you have become dull of hearing. For though by this time you ought to be teachers, you need someone to teach you again the basic principles of the oracles of God. You need milk, not solid food, for everyone who lives on milk is unskilled in the word of righteousness, since he is a child. But solid food is for the mature, for those who have

their powers of discernment trained by constant practice to distinguish good from evil." Hebrews 5:11-14

The author here has set up the direct target audience, he is showing us the intended audience is immature, unskilled, dull of hearing (the word), needing more milk, and should be more advanced by now. Friends, the target audience for these verses is absolutely **not** mature!! Again, this group is primarily heart types 1 and 2.

Yet, many would now repeat verses 4-6 to me and tell me that these are *mature* believers:

*"⁴ For it is impossible, in the case of those who have once been enlightened, who have tasted the heavenly gift, and have shared in the Holy Spirit, ⁵ and have tasted the goodness of the word of God and the powers of the age to come, ⁶ and then have **fallen away**, to restore them again to repentance" Hebrews 6:4-6* (emphasis added for clarity)

These are believers who have been taught, shown Truth, tasted the goodness of God, have received from the Holy Spirit (healing, prophecy) and witnessed the power of the Holy Spirit at work in others ... but decided the gospel wasn't for them. Again, if they have *fallen away* from persecution, they are in ***heart type two*** according to the parable of the sower (Matthew 13:21).

What's more, Paul describes the mature believers as those who are hungry for the things of God (Philippians 3:10-16) ... so how would they suddenly just decide to leave Jesus??

Friends, here is what I love so much about **Hebrews 6:1-8,** it's really a repeat of the parable of the sower: "*For land that has drunk the rain that often falls on it, and produces a*

LEAVING THE 99

crop useful to those for whose sake it is cultivated, receives a blessing from God." Hebrews 6:7

Yes, the author is describing the four heart types!! He even says the heart type with the thorns and thistles choking the seed are destined for the fire ... *"But if it bears thorns and thistles, it is worthless and near to being cursed, and its end is to be burned." Hebrews 6:8*

So, I would say heart type **three** is a case by case basis. Not all in this heart type are saved!!!! A warning would do some in this group good!

Furthermore, people fail to read the very next set of verses:

"Though we speak in this way, yet in your case, beloved, we feel sure of better things—things that belong to salvation. For God is not unjust so as to overlook your work and the love that you have shown for his name in serving the saints, as you still do." Hebrews 6:9-10

After warning them about eternal judgment, the author then tells this group that he is sure and certain of far better things that <u>belong to salvation</u> ... because those in heart types 3 and 4 have nothing to fear!!

One last misinterpreted verse I'd like to cover from 2 Peter:

"For if, after they have escaped the defilements of the world through the knowledge of our Lord and Savior Jesus Christ, they are again entangled in them and overcome, the last state has become worse for them than the first. [21] For it would have been better for them never to have known the way of righteousness than after knowing it to turn back from the holy commandment delivered to them." 2 Peter 2:20-21

Alan Caplin

This verse is written about *false teachers!* Yes, those who knew the Truth, but chose to reject the Truth! What's more, Jude tells us that these false teachers and false prophets do **not** have the Holy Spirit (Jude 1:19). They have a demonic spirit, not the Holy Spirit! This verse has nothing to do with a saved believer!

Simply put, if Jesus loses forever heartfelt, spirit born sons and daughters ... then God's covenant of hope, peace, life, freedom, protection, and salvation ... is 100% worthless.

"I give them eternal life, and they will never perish, and no one will snatch them out of my hand." John 10:28

"I will not violate my covenant or alter the word that went forth from my lips." Psalm 89:34

A friend of mine was once in prayer about the promises of The Lord and the new covenant. I have never forgotten what she had written to me, for it has been emblazoned on my heart as truth.

SHE HEARD THE LORD SAY, "YOU WERE NOT THERE WHEN I MADE THIS COVENANT. IT IS BY MYSELF THAT IT IS ESTABLISHED AND CARRIED OUT. THEREFORE, THOUGH ONE MAY WALK AWAY – THE COVENANT CANNOT BE BROKEN BY ANYONE BUT ME. I AM FAITHFUL. AND EVEN WHEN MY CHILDREN ARE UNFAITHFUL, I REMAIN FAITHFUL. MY KINDNESS LEADS TO REPENTANCE. MY LOVE IS IRRESISTIBLE."

LEAVING THE 99

A Living Sacrifice

*"I appeal to you therefore, brothers, by the mercies of God, to present your **bodies** as a **living sacrifice**, holy and acceptable to God, which is your spiritual worship. Do not be <u>conformed</u> to this world, but be <u>transformed</u> by the **renewal of your <u>mind</u>**, that by testing you may discern what is the will of God, what is good and acceptable and perfect." Romans 12:1-2* (emphasis added for clarity)

The only way for the human body to be offered as a living sacrifice, is if the heart and mind are ***both*** willing. Each day we have the choice to either *conform* into the image of the world or to *transform* into the image of Christ. One is death, and one is life.

This is why Paul says to renew the thoughts of the mind, so our soul (*heart and mind*) can transform into the image (soul) of Christ. This word for "mind" in the Greek (*nous*) isn't referring to your ***brain***. Rather, the word "mind" is referring to the ***soul*** (heart ***and*** mind). The heart and mind both think!!!! To mature, our thoughts must be constantly realigned with Truth and The Holy Spirit.

*"For who has understood the **mind (nous)** of the Lord so as to instruct him?" But <u>we</u> have the **mind (nous)** of Christ. 1 Corinthians 2:16* (emphasis and nous added)

We have the mind **(nous: soul)** of Jesus, and we are able to tap into His perfect mind **(nous: soul)** for instruction and direction! Yes! We are able to *think* just like He does! Friends, we have been designed to experience the **soul realm** of free will, thought, and emotion just like He did here on earth!

We must continue to transform so our soul can catch up to our perfect spirit! Yet, Paul instructs that we are no longer to regard *any* believer by the flesh (soul, body), but rather by the Spirit. If you are in covenant with Jesus, you are a **new creation,** a spirit born entity!

"From now on, therefore, we regard no one according to the flesh. Even though we once regarded Christ according to the flesh, we regard him thus no longer. Therefore, if anyone is in Christ, he is a new creation. The old has passed away; behold, the new has come."
2 Corinthians 5:16-17

Because you live from the Spirit, the impossible is to be your **new normal.** What isn't possible from the flesh, will always be possible by the Spirit. If The Lord instructs you straight into the impossible, then it is *fully* possible!

The only thing blocking your path, is your soul and your unbelief. This is why Jesus killed your soul! You died!!!

*"Whoever seeks to preserve his **life (psyche: soul)** will lose it, but whoever loses his **life (psyche: soul)** will keep it." Luke 17:33* (emphasis and psyche added for clarity)

The more we try to keep things our own way or to control our situations, the less peace we will have within our own soul. But, the more we <u>rest</u> and lose our soul for kingdom, the more peace we will have within our soul. True rest is a product of both faith and trust in Jesus ... and this is the only way to really keep the health of the soul. Otherwise, we are dependent on self.

Honestly, because we have been created and purposed to be like Jesus in every way ... it is **now** time for the **Body of Christ** to have our faith, hearts, and limits tested.

LEAVING THE 99

The best way I can explain the testing of limits is by using a scene from the movie *"Top Gun: Maverick" (2022)*.

Maverick arrives the first day to teach his highly skilled class of fighter pilots, and he holds up the manual for the aircraft while saying, "I'm assuming you know the book inside and out."

They all raise their hands with great confidence, and he throws the manual in the trash can. Maverick says, "So does your enemy. But what the enemy doesn't know is your limits. I intend to find them, test them, push beyond. Today we will start with what you think you know. You show me what you are made of."

The devil has read the Bible. He knows exactly what you are purposed for and how you *should* operate. He knows how you are wired, and he knows what on-board weapons you have!!!

This is why he hates Christ in you. Yet, our true limits are being tested in order to increase skill, power, confidence, teamwork, purpose, faith, boldness, endurance, surrender, self-sacrifice, and our maneuverability against the plans of the enemy (Hebrews 12:26-29).

Our limits are being tested with:

Politics/national leadership/fraud
Finances/interest rates/inflation
Gas/food prices/healthcare costs
Item supply/affordable housing
Church/faith
Covid/death
Friendships/isolation
Corruption/injustice

Alan Caplin

Court decisions/social issues
Anger/hate/riots/defund the police
Decay of morality/family chaos
Global war/irrationality

As pressure or the g-force upon you increases, go beyond what the aircraft manual says you can do. You are called to greater. You are called to more. You are called to fight!

Jesus is the best of the best - and so are you in covenant with Him. You are made from His DNA – you are made in His image. Yes. It's time for our highly skilled pilots and fighter jets to take off in order to do the impossible against the schemes of the enemy!

"but just as we have been approved by God to be entrusted with the gospel, so we speak, not to please man, but to please God who tests our hearts." 1 Thess 2:4

"for you know that the testing of your faith produces steadfastness." James 1:3

The same way that John the Baptist prepared the way for Jesus, we are to do the same for The Second Coming of Christ (*Isaiah 61:1-11*). John was willing to lay his own life down to pave that way. I'm very sorry. But. The true gospel teaches us that we are expected for the same commitment. Friends, prepare the way of The Lord.

I'd like to add, many love to talk about Jezebel, but few are willing to confront her. If you have ever been hated, threatened, harassed, misunderstood, bullied, controlled, or been afraid of someone's unkind remarks or thoughts about you ... this condensed story of **1 Kings 19** is for you.

LEAVING THE 99

Elijah operated in great power, saw miraculous, and made the name of The Lord greatly known in the presence of His enemies (Baal). Angry Jezebel threatens to kill Elijah, and Elijah fearfully runs away into the desert. Elijah is so worn out from fear that he wishes he could just lay down and die. Then, an angel of The Lord (pre-incarnate Jesus) comes to feed, hydrate, strengthen, and restore Elijah.

The angel says, *"Arise and eat, for the journey is too great for you."* Yes. The angel (Jesus) knows the choice Elijah is making.

In that very moment, Elijah had a choice to continue on for 40 days and 40 nights of suffering towards the cave at Mt. Horeb - or - to return to His assignment taking on the prophets of Baal and Jezebel. Afraid, he goes on ahead to the cave, and upon arrival, The Lord says, *"What are you doing here, Elijah?"*

Yes, The Lord fed and restored Elijah and <u>allowed</u> Elijah to keep running ahead to the cave. Then, his God given prophetic assignment was **stripped**: *"Elisha the son of Shaphat of Abel-meholah you shall anoint to be prophet in your place."* 1 Kings 19:16

Once The Lord refreshes us from difficulty and gets us back on our feet, we have a choice. To either be a son or to cower in fear. We can choose to run from those who have hurt us, or we can choose to go back and be Jesus to them. We can choose to follow through with our kingdom assignment, or we can choose to relinquish it to another.

Despite it all, The Lord took Elijah right up in a chariot and Elijah never, ever tasted death. That's how much he loved Elijah. He loves you too. He loves you right where you are and in the choices you've made. But, He wants to see you fully trust in Him to empower you in getting your kingdom assignment *completed*.

Fear will always be the thief of destiny, and many have sadly run from theirs.

"When I am afraid,
I put my trust in you.
In God, whose word I praise,
in God I trust; I shall not be afraid.
What can flesh do to me?"
Psalm 56:3-4

I honestly believe that our response to The Lord's leading often depends on our own interpretation of these 3 words **"It is finished"** (John 19:30).

What was finished? I love how the heart of man gets to interpret this verse. So vague, yet so very powerful. Scan social media theology and you will see how many *false grace* people make this into an anthem of how we have nothing to do. The Lord has done it all ... without us.

Yet. Moments before Jesus tasted death, Jesus announces *"It is finished"* and if we go over to Hebrews 2:14-15 we see ***who*** was finished ...

*"Since therefore the children share in flesh and blood, he himself likewise partook of the same things, that through death he might destroy the **one** who has the **power of death**, that is, **the devil**, and **deliver all those who through fear of death were subject to lifelong slavery**."*
Hebrews 2:14-15 (emphasis added for clarity)

Yep, the devil was finished! The devil was destroyed, along with the entire system of law, sin, **and** death. The

LEAVING THE 99

debt of sin and legal requirements of the law had been nailed to the cross (Colossians 2:13-15). The system of law was *finished* for training unto righteousness, and the devil was finished too!

The devil no longer holds the keys and power over death, Jesus does! Written to the Jewish believers running back to the temple due to persecution ... the victory at the cross means those who fear death, no longer need to be slave to that lifelong fear! Too many believers fear death, because they have no idea that they are *alive*!

At the cross, the path was paved for you and I to take back every single ounce of territory that the devil has stolen from the sons and daughters of The Lord. **AND**, everything we will ever do in His name, as led by His Spirit, was *already* provided for and completed *before* time itself began.

"his works were finished from the foundation of the world." Hebrews 4:3

The Lord sits **outside** time – everything in the earth is playing out before Him at the same time. Past, present, and future are all happening together at the same time! The work in you, for you, and through you is ***finished*** because it's already ***been*** done! Yes, The Lord always knows the end from the beginning (Isaiah 46:9-10).

In **covenant** with the best of the best, friends, let's take off together into the unknown. As led by The Spirit, let's be willing to return to incomplete assignments and let's be willing to accept new assignments. Let's trust Him! Let's take back what's been stolen. Let's be the living sacrifice and prepare the way for The Lord!

Alan Caplin

The Two Anointings

Religion and *legalism* will often focus on bringing the Holy Spirit down from heaven to the exclusion of The Spirit within, and *false gracism* will focus on the Spirit within to the exclusion of The Holy Spirit resting upon.

Friends, we need both! The Holy Spirit within and upon are *some* of the tools The Lord gives us to get kingdom work done.

What saddens me is that in both the *legalism* and *false gracism* camps, many think they have been baptized in the Holy Spirit because they speak in tongues, that's just not true. And because they think they have all they are ever going to get .... they stop pursuing God and stop receiving the **more of God**. Yes, they stay stuck!

Me, I was speaking in tongues and seeing people healed of many things before I was baptized in the Holy Spirit. In fact, I was given a gift of healing over 25 years ago - long before I knew anything about doctrine, scripture, or church!

There are 2 separate anointings:

1. Within
2. Upon

The very moment you believe from your heart, you are fused to heaven. Your spirit and the Holy Spirit are now one, you are a new creation (2 Corinthians 5:17). Your human spirit or candle (Proverbs 20:27) has been lit by

LEAVING THE 99

The Spirit of The Lord. You have *within* you access to all of heaven, giftings that reside or live in your belly can be activated, and the same power sits inside you that raised Christ from the dead.

You have received the free gift of eternal salvation, and your human spirit (or inner being) has been made alive. You, as a new creation, now dwell in the forever and this *within* is for you (Colossians 2:13, 1 Corinthians 6:17; Ephesians 2:5 and 3:16; Philippians 2:1; Romans 6:3).

Upon, is the baptism of the Holy Spirit and power (Acts 1:8; 10:38). This anointing is for others and the work of ministry. **AND**, you can receive *multiple* baptisms in the Holy Spirit. See Acts 4:31 where Peter and John (with some friends) receive again and Acts 13:52 where Paul and Barnabas receive again.

In fact, the original disciples received the upon *prior* to the cross (Luke 9:1), they received *again* at Pentecost (Acts 2:4), and both Peter and John received *again* after dealing with threats of death from the Jewish elite (Acts 4:31). Peter and John, had *at least* 3 documented events of the Holy Spirit falling upon them!

Here is the thing, this stuff really shouldn't insult anyone because Paul never settled. He was constantly seeking to know Jesus more and the power of the resurrection. Paul constantly was seeking more of God to flow through him, for others (Philippians 3:10-16).

Too many believers, either out of ignorance or unbelief, sit in a passive comfort zone and settle for less than they can receive. Yet, others refuse to move off their duff until they are convinced they have all they are going to get.

Alan Caplin

Both views are anti-faith.
Both views are anti-christ.

Like it or not, we are under a law of faith (Romans 3:27-31) and the righteous will live by this faith. Yes. All we do is fueled by faith working itself through love, and we walk out that which God will work out. Folks, the more we receive our death, the more we can receive life. Jesus didn't settle, nor should we.

Yes, *within and upon*, we actually have a biblical account where we can see the clear difference in the two.

"Now when the apostles at Jerusalem heard that Samaria had received the word of God, they sent to them Peter and John, who came down and prayed for them that they might receive the Holy Spirit, for he had not yet fallen on any of them, but they had only been baptized in the name of the Lord Jesus. Then they laid their hands on them and they received the Holy Spirit." Acts 8:14-17

The Samaritans had been baptized into the **name of The Lord Jesus** ... this is **BOTH** the water baptism *and* being immersed into the death and life of Jesus (Romans 6:3). From belief and belief alone, this is where the Samaritans received salvation and the within!

Then some time later, Peter and John both came to pray for them and they received the Holy Spirit upon! Unlike most biblical accounts, there was a distinct difference in the timing of the two anointings.

Yet, out of the overflow of the upon comes the boldness of Acts 4 ... and the unrestraint of the world! This is why we often confuse the *"when"* of the baptism of the Holy Spirit - for those who hunger after the kingdom and His

LEAVING THE 99

Righteousness (Jesus) - we are *always* experiencing the power of more upon us.

I'd like to use an analogy, I love analogies! Let's look at solar panels for a moment. Solar panels lay flat on the roof ... doing absolutely nothing! They have no power source of their own and have zero moving parts – they just receive, store, and redistribute power from the sun.

The panels announce to the rays of the sun, "Land here and please use me for distribution to the working elements of the home." The toaster, the refrigerator, the microwave, the oven, the hairdryer, the computer, and all else powered in that home depend on the panel source *upon* the roof.

This is where many believers get confused over the within and upon. The second you believe, you have the power of heaven within you - accessible and operated *by faith*. By the Spirit, you now have the ability to raise the dead! Yes, we all have the same power within us, but we don't all respond with the same faith. Hence, a variety of results!

But, the upon. This is the difference maker.

We don't all have the same amount of the Holy Spirit upon us as Jesus did. Those baptized in the Holy Spirit all have varying degrees of His Spirit resting upon them. Some do have more than others. If we had the same upon as Jesus, we'd need to have the same moral character to sustain the massive responsibilities of this power. But, this is available to us *by faith*.

*"For he **(Jesus)** whom God has sent utters the words of God, for he **(Jesus)** gives the Spirit without measure." John 3:34* (emphasis and **Jesus** added by me for clarity)

Alan Caplin

- When you know you died.
- When you know to surrender.
- When you know you're alive to redistribute power.

When you fully lay down your life and are willing to give yourself up for the toaster and refrigerator. Then, you are in great position to receive *more of The Spirit* upon from the Son. Yes, with great power stored, alive only for service - The Holy Spirit on His own uses what's stored *in* and *upon* you. You merely become a conduit, often unaware of what the Spirit is doing in others around you.

Like the Ark resting on Mt. Ararat, The Holy Spirit simply rests upon you and does the work of the ministry. As Jesus is right now, so am I and so are you (1 John 4:17).

Honestly, the church has an incorrect view of what it means to be filled with the Spirit, which is often a huge reason the church sits stagnant.

As my friend Aymeric Bimont clearly points out, you aren't a bottle filled with water. Rather, you are the main sail on a sailboat. Bottles are stagnant and non-moving. Living water cannot flow through a bottle with a closed lid (John 7:38)!

But. Sails are filled with life!

Sails wait patiently for the wind.
Sails learn the ways of the wind.
Sails romance and dance with the wind.
Sails must participate to receive the wind.
Sails are powerless without the wind.
Sails go where taken and have no agenda.

And sails are constantly filled. Over and over!

LEAVING THE 99

*Paul writes, "And do not get drunk with wine, for that is debauchery, but be filled **(plēroō)** with the Spirit." Ephesians 5:18* (emphasis and plēroō added for clarity)

From Blue Letter Bible App:
plēroō - to make full, to fill up, fill to full
passive tense - receiving *from* God
present tense - continuing action, something that happens continuously or repeatedly

The Holy Spirit is *constantly* upon you. We must always seek Him ... and perpetually receive a refreshing wind!

Friends, the Father wants to give us more. He wants us to **believe** there is more! Yes! It is His good pleasure to give us the riches, treasure, and wealth of kingdom power ... but we first have to want it! We must seek the kingdom! Our treasure will be wherever our heart is, and The Lord desires our hearts to be intently focused on things above not on things below here in the earth (Luke 12:29-34).

*"Blessed be the God and Father of our Lord Jesus Christ, who **has** blessed us **in Christ** with **every** spiritual blessing in the heavenly places" Ephesians 1:3* (emphasis added)

In covenant with Jesus, we already possess every spiritual blessing. Yes, this spiritual blessing is already ours in the spirit realm ... we simply access our inheritance by faith!

"In him we have obtained an inheritance, having been predestined according to the purpose of him who works all things according to the counsel of his will, so that we who were the first to hope in Christ might be to the praise of his glory. In him you also, when you heard the word of truth, the gospel of your salvation, and believed in him, were sealed with the promised Holy Spirit, who is the

guarantee of our inheritance until we acquire possession of it, to the praise of his glory." Ephesians 1:11-14

Friends, your heart has been forever marked by The Holy Spirit as being the **property** of The Lord. And this mark of The Spirit is the **guarantee** of our **inheritance UNTIL** we acquire possession of it!!!!!! This acquisition of full inheritance could be today, tomorrow, next month, or in heaven ... but *by faith* we keep seeking and hungering!

Very few believers understand the reality of *mustard seed faith*. It's one of those things we kind of take for granted.

*He put another parable before them, saying, "The kingdom of heaven is like a grain of mustard seed that a man took and sowed in his field. It is the **SMALLEST** of all seeds, but when it has **GROWN** it is larger than all the garden plants and **BECOMES A TREE**, so that the birds of the air come and make **NESTS** in its branches." Matthew 13:31-32* (emphasis added for clarity)

First, the tree grows. This is a basic principle of kingdom. We never arrive and are always becoming more and more like Jesus. In fact, even Jesus grew ... Jesus went into the desert **full** of the Spirit (or filled with the Spirit), but He came out of the desert 40 days later in the **POWER** of the Spirit (Luke 4:1; 4:14).

But, here is the mind blower. A mustard seed is really an *herb*. It's a plant, *not* a tree! Yet, it becomes a tree. The plant *seeks* to be *more*! The mustard seed is the smallest of all seeds, and as a seed, is meant to "just" be a spice or herb. Yet despite limitations ... the mustard seed grows, transcends, and transforms to become much greater than an herb or plant.

LEAVING THE 99

Truly, this mustard seed becomes far larger than a garden plant to be a place of *rest* for those who seek refuge and a place to nest away from the world. For a *plant* to become a *tree*, it must first take on a full-scale identity change in order to become greater. You were born into Adam, born into both death and darkness. However, taking on our full identity in Christ ... we must in fact choose to *grow* as the seed that Jesus Himself has sown into the earth.

He answered, "The one who sows the good seed is the Son of Man. The field is the world, and the good seed is the sons of the kingdom" (Matthew 13:37-38).

Jesus is sowing exact replicas of Himself into the earth. We transform from death to life, from darkness to light, from self to selflessness, and from sons of disobedience to sons of the kingdom. In covenant with Christ, we are called to **ALL** Jesus did ... and greater.

At one point in my journey, I was very unsure if I had His giftings sitting inside of me. I wasn't seeing some things manifest, so I had questioned if they were there. But, The Lord gave me an amazing revelation at my school. It was Superhero Day, and I got to wear my Captain America outfit! I was wearing the padded muscle costume and I had been admiring the added bulk around my chest ... but not wanting to invest time into adding the actual muscle.

The PE teacher had been standing right there smiling and he says to me, "You do realize that all those muscles are already inside you?"

Immediately, all the lights went off in my head! Whether I choose to work them into visible development or not, the muscles *are* there. Even if nobody can **SEE** them ... they are *still* there! So too are our spiritual giftings!

These gifts are **already** inside you. But are you willing to walk these things out by faith? Are you willing to work these skills into some type of shape? Are you willing to risk some embarrassment by working out in the Gym of The Holy Spirit to flex muscle in the spirit realm?

Friends, you can't be used to heal the sick if you are afraid to lay hands. You can't speak in tongues or share prophetic words if you don't ever spend time with God to learn how to release the language and promises of heaven. You can't understand the word of God, if you never spend time **in** the word of God. And you surely can't hear God's voice if you talk more than you listen.

We must stop jealously desiring the muscles of others, when the powerful muscles already sit inside you.

Now, I do want to add that despite giftings sitting within you ... I very much do believe ***impartation*** and ***activation*** are real things. I have received this way too many times to discount it as truth and I've prayed for others receiving this too many times as well.

But, until recently, I've never had a verse to confidently point to and say, "yep, it is written and there it is!"

"For this reason I remind you to fan into flame the gift of God, which is in you through the laying on of my hands, for God gave us a spirit not of fear but of power and love and self-control." 2 Timothy 1:6

That gift of God I have always read as the gift of the Holy Spirit. I've always read that verse as Paul saying he laid his hands on Timothy and he received the deposit within of the Holy Spirit. Well, that makes no sense because the within or union with Holy Spirit comes at the point of belief and not from the laying of human hands.

Yet, the Spirit *upon* often comes with the laying of hands. So, here in the laying of hands, what was the specific gift that Timothy received?

We go to the previous 2 sentences.

> *"As I remember your tears, I long to see you, that I may be filled with joy. I am reminded of your sincere **faith**, a **faith** that dwelt first in your grandmother Lois and your mother Eunice and now, **I am sure, dwells in you as well**."*
> 2 Timothy 1:4-5 (emphasis added for clarity)

In the laying of hands, Timothy received an activation of the gift of faith. The same gift his mom and grandma had.

Let me say this. When someone prays for impartation over another person, what is received depends fully upon God and what God wants to do in that moment - not what we personally want to see happen. I've seen people suddenly receive great power or great gifting, and I've seen people receive peace, joy, hope, boldness, patience, faith, or new strength.

I remember a friend once prayed over me for impartation and I saw a flat bicycle tire being filled with new air. I was receiving fresh strength and stability. Yet, at times I've felt my entire belly move, and I've seen The Lord place special things in my hands. No matter what is received, we receive exactly what we need from God in that particular moment. Regardless, impartation by the Spirit isn't to be disregarded as "a thing" and impartation isn't a shortcut to the character growth necessary for true maturity.

Alan Caplin

Don't chase the gift. Chase the Giver! Whatever you need, will manifest when it is <u>*supposed*</u> to (1 Cor 12:4-11).

I'd like to add this random thought, many mistake this verse below to mean that you can lose your salvation. Others who serve Jesus live in fear that they might be dismissed by The Lord when they leave earth.

"Not everyone who says to me, 'Lord, Lord,' will enter the kingdom of heaven, but the one who does the will of my Father who is in heaven. On that day many will say to me, 'Lord, Lord, did we not prophesy in your name, and cast out demons in your name, and do many mighty works in your name?' And then will I declare to them, 'I never knew you; depart from me, you workers of lawlessness.' Matthew 7:21-23

This verse is referring to false ministers of the gospel who are operating from the *upon*, but do not have the *within*.

"And no wonder, for even Satan disguises himself as an angel of light. So it is no surprise if his servants, also, disguise themselves as servants of righteousness. Their end will correspond to their deeds." 2 Cor 11:14-15

Remember, these false workers of light are just like Judas. Judas, like the other 11 disciples, operated in great power *upon* – but Judas wasn't in the locked room to receive the *within* after the resurrection. Yes, The Lord will even use the wicked to move the gospel, but their end will fit their self-motivated deeds.

A couple of last thoughts on seeking the treasure of heaven. The path to these riches will rarely be a straight line and there is **no treasure map**! Each and every person will have a different path, and I guarantee there will be opposition from

LEAVING THE 99

friends, family, the church, and from the devil. There will be days you want to quit and there will be days you are on top of the world. There will even be days that you question your sanity ... been there! Yet, what you are seeking **WILL** come to pass, if you don't give up (Galatians 6:9).

Remember, keep sowing to the Spirit. Keep sowing into the spirit realm, for that's where His life is! That's where your growth is, and that's where your treasure is! Yes, the Spirit is where eternal life begins and *never* ends!

"For the one who sows to his own flesh will from the flesh reap corruption, but the one who sows to the Spirit will from the Spirit reap eternal life. And let us not grow weary of doing good, for in due season we will reap, if we do not give up." Galatians 6:8-9

Friends, the only way to see manifestation of the Spirit on the outside, is to first see it on the **inside**! Dare to imagine with The Lord, dare to dream, dare to allow His plans to fill your heart. See His desires through the eyes of your heart!

The word hope in the Greek is elpis, and this word means to expect or anticipate. Literally, hope is an *expectation*!!

*"To them God chose to make known how great among the Gentiles are the **riches of the glory** of this mystery, which is Christ **in** you, the **hope (expectation) of glory**." Colossians 1:27* (emphasis and expectation added)

The Lord showing up through you isn't a wish or fantasy. Rather it is the ***desire of The Lord***! Expect Him to reveal His glory (light; presence) both within you and through you, and don't *ever* quit because the blessing is too great! While you wait and persevere, transform (Romans 8:18)!

Alan Caplin

Elijah and The Double Portion

The newly recruited disciples turn to Jesus and say, *"so, where are you staying?"* And Jesus says to them, *"come and you will see."*

That word "staying" is menō or to ***abide***. Jesus had told the disciples where He was staying ... abiding and remaining unshakable in the Father. We need to stay right where Jesus stayed - in the place of unshakeable! In that place of rest and abiding in the Father, Jesus was inviting His friends into a life where they could do everything that He did. Jesus was putting out the invitation for His new recruits to live from surrender ... and to do the impossible.

Come follow Jesus and you will see.

"Jesus turned and saw them following and said to them, "What are you seeking?" And they said to him, "Rabbi", "where are you staying?" He said to them, "Come and you will see." So they came and saw where he was staying, and they stayed with him that day, for it was about the tenth hour." John 1:38-39

You too are His recruits. You too are His disciples. You too have the invitation to do what Jesus did.

Every miracle.
Every person healed.
Every demon cast out.
Every resurrection encounter.
Every life touched.
Every disciple recruited and grown.
Every sermon taught.

LEAVING THE 99

Every ministerial moment.
Every insult received.
Every tear shed.
Every betrayal weathered.
Every temptation withstood.
Every threat burdened or shouldered.
Every storm stopped.
Every physical threat evaded.
Every enemy or hater blessed.
Every woman at the well moment.
Every ounce of pain on the cross.

Was done, as a man. Jesus refers to Himself over 80 times in the gospels as The Son of Man - which means human or messiah. Jesus humbled Himself by choosing to strip off His own divinity - and walk out His earthly mission as a human being, *not* as God (Philippians 2:1-11).

- That makes Jesus our role model.
- That makes Jesus our reachable target.
- That makes us containers awaiting His own power.

Friends, the more we embrace our co-death, co-burial, co-resurrection, and co-ascension ... the more we can love on others at the expense of self.

My wife, Lori, once shared a revelation with me that I find fascinating. The word for tongue in Hebrew (לְשׁוֹן l'shone) has a value of 386 in the Gematria, and the mathematical value of 386 is equal to ... **YESHUA!**

- Your tongue carries the same weight as Jesus!

- Your tongue was designed to carry the authority of Jesus!

Alan Caplin

- Your tongue is weaponized straight from the throne to speak forth life and healing!

- Your tongue has positioned you as a co-creator with Jesus!

Every word you say has the power to usher in death or life.

"Death and life are in the power of the tongue, and those who love it will eat its fruits." Proverbs 18:21

Jesus cursed the fig tree, it withered.
Jesus blessed people, freedom came.
Jesus spoke healing, wholeness crashed in.

"Behold, I have given you authority to tread on serpents and scorpions, and over all the power of the enemy, and nothing shall hurt you." Luke 10:19

Jesus has given us His authority to trample on the enemy!! But many believers don't understand **how** to operate in His authority. I'd like to share this simple story and analogy.

I was subbing for a 5th grade teacher, and I made a student named "Seth" in charge of the entire class. Seth was tiny, tiny. I made Seth the teacher for the day and I told him he had the power to take away recess, to give extra homework, and to give lunch detention. The kid looked at me like I was *crazy*. How were these other kids going to listen to him?

While Seth was teaching the lesson ... I took off my necktie and I placed it around his own neck. I had stood behind him with my arms crossed the entire time he was in front of the class ... and you know what ... there wasn't one peep in the room. Why? He was operating in **MY** authority.

LEAVING THE 99

It is no different with Jesus! He stands alongside us, within us, and upon us with His power and authority ... we simply operate in Him! Yes, Jesus has given us His authority over darkness! When we believe it, we can walk in it!

"And these signs will accompany those who believe: in my name they will cast out demons; they will speak in new tongues; they will pick up serpents with their hands; and if they drink any deadly poison, it will not hurt them; they will lay their hands on the sick, and they will recover." Mark 16:17-18

As believers, these are our basic rights! Because *you* believe *you* are able to cast out devils, speak in new tongues, easily survive very deadly situations, and lay hands to see the sick recover. But, when we dig far deeper into the words of the **_prophets_** and deeper into the words of Jesus ... we have the right to so much more! You have the right to the *inheritance of the first born* ... stay with me here, you will be amazed.

"O foolish ones, and slow of heart to believe all that the prophets have spoken!" Luke 24:25

One of my favorite sections of scripture comes from **Mark 10:35-45**. The Sons of Thunder, James and John, are **_with_** the *other 10 disciples* and right in front of them, they boldly say to Jesus, *"Grant us to sit, one at your right hand and one at your left, in your glory."* Jesus, in an almost baffled tone, then responds, *"You do not know what you are asking. Are you able to drink the cup that I drink, or to be baptized with the baptism with which I am baptized?"*

Jesus is literally asking them if they are able to drink the same cup of suffering and able to be baptized in the same measure of The Holy Spirit that Jesus was baptized with.

James and John kind of take a look at one another, think for a second, and then respond back, *"We are able."*

To the anger and bewilderment of the other 10, these 2 guys were just told in effect, "ok you will suffer like I will suffer, and you will walk in the same power that I walk in."

Jesus then tells the 12, *"But whoever would be great among you must be your servant, and whoever would be first among you must be slave of all. For even the Son of Man came not to be served but to serve, and to give his life as a ransom for many."*

Jesus is telling them they *are* able to walk the same way Jesus did, *if* they are willing to walk in full surrender. To be truly great they had to be the servant of others. To be *first* among them, they had to be the *slave* of *all*. If they would be willing to give their own lives as a ransom – then they too could be baptized (immersed) in the same measure of The Holy Spirit. The measure *upon* them would be directly proportional to their self-sacrifice!! (John 3:34)

Jesus is telling us that **YES**, we too have the same right. We have the same opportunity!! Folks, we have to see it on the inside and then we will begin to see it on the outside!!! One of the disciples asked Jesus to teach them how to pray, and Jesus goes through the portion we all know:

"Father, hallowed be your name. Your kingdom come. Give us each day our daily bread, and forgive us our sins, for we ourselves forgive everyone who is indebted to us. And lead us not into temptation." Luke 11:2-4

But we miss the next section of *"how to pray"* – and this is the *key* to *everything*! Jesus tells us the story of a man who had a guest come over late at night, and the man wanted to

LEAVING THE 99

provide *3* loaves of bread (Father, Son, and Holy Spirit) to this friend who had traveled a great distance. It's midnight, this traveler came suddenly, and the man wanted to both honor and feed him. So he boldly bangs on his neighbor's door for bread and the man inside gives it to him – not for their friendship – but rather for his **persistence** to **bless his friend** who just came from a long journey! *Luke 11:5-8*

Remember, this is still part of The Lord's prayer. This is how we *ought* to pray! Jesus says,

"And I tell you, ask, and it will be given to you; seek, and you will find; knock, and it will be opened to you. For everyone who asks receives, and the one who seeks finds, and to the one who knocks it will be opened." Luke 11:9-10

If we ask, if we **seek** *(yes, leave the 99 to go on a journey for His treasure),* and if we knock on the door – the door *will* be opened. Watch this, ***what is this door to???***

"If you then, who are evil, know how to give good gifts to your children, how much more will the heavenly Father give the Holy Spirit to those who ask him!" Luke 11:13

Friends, that door is the door to **The Holy Spirit**!!! And, the door opens simply because He desires to bless you, so you can bless others! This man who boldly banged on the door to The Holy Spirit at midnight for bread (Jesus), was doing this for **SOMEONE else**! Yes, we seek the power and the more of Jesus, so we can *feed* the needs of others!!!!

Yes, it is our right as co-heirs to have the same measure of The Holy Spirit upon us as Jesus, and yes maybe even more than He had (John 14:12)! But, from the words and actions of the Old Testament prophets, I want to show you our legal inheritance right ... ***the right of the first born.***

Alan Caplin

At the transfiguration, Moses and Elijah had been talking with Jesus (Matthew 17:3). This is just before Jesus is to go to the cross, be resurrected, and ascend to The Father. The three men are probably talking strategy here, but Moses and Elijah are representative of **the law** and the **prophets**. All that had been written in the Old Testament pointed to Jesus and to this very moment of the cross (Matthew 11:13).

Elijah was a symbol of **every prophetic word** written by each and every prophet. Elijah is a picture of the promises of The Lord!

Elisha was a prophetic symbol of Jesus. Elisha had worked many miracles that had been similar to Jesus. Elisha had raised the dead (2 Kings 4:33-35), produced an abundance of oil from a small amount (2 Kings 4:1-7), cured Naaman of leprosy (2 Kings 5:1-14), and he fed 100 men from 20 loaves of bread (2 Kings 4:42-43).

Elijah represents the **promises** of The Lord. While, **Elisha** represents the **receiving of promises,** specifically promises of the *right of the first born or the double portion*! Stay with me, your chin will drop!

Remember, after running from Jezebel and ending up in the cave The Lord told Elijah to anoint Elisha as prophet. Elijah ***immediately*** did so as he *"passed by him and cast his cloak upon him." 1 Kings 19:19*

Some time later, Elijah is about to be taken up in a chariot of fire, but before he is to leave, Elijah tells Elisha, *"Ask what I shall do for you, before I am taken from you." And Elisha said, "Please let there be a **double portion** of your spirit on me." And he said, "You have asked a **hard thing**; yet, **if you see me** as I am being taken from you, it*

LEAVING THE 99

shall be so for you, but if you do not see me, it shall not be so." 2 Kings 2:9-10 (emphasis added)

Elijah asks Elisha what he could do for him before he departs and Elisha boldly asks for a double portion of Elijah's spirit. Elijah replies this is a **hard thing** he has asked. But, if you **SEE ME** as I am leaving, then it will happen. But, if you ***don't*** see me, then it won't happen.

*"And Elijah went up by a whirlwind into heaven. And Elisha **SAW IT** and he cried, "My father, my father! The chariots of Israel and its horsemen!" And he saw him no more. Then he took hold of his own clothes and tore them in two pieces. And **he took up the cloak of Elijah that had fallen from him** and went back and stood on the bank of the Jordan."* 2 Kings 2:11-13 (emphasis added)

ELISHA, THE <u>RECIPIENT</u> OF THE WRITTEN OLD TESTAMENT PROMISES, <u>SAW</u> THE PROMISES OF THE PROPHETS AS THE PROMISES HAD BEEN TAKEN INTO HEAVEN AWAITING JESUS!!!!!!!

Elisha saw the promises of The Lord and he had received a *second* anointing upon of Elijah's spirit. Yes, Elisha had received *the more*, but *<u>what exactly is a double portion?</u>*

It's right of the first born son! Jesus! In ancient Israel, the family inheritance wasn't split up evenly. The first born son always received *<u>double</u>* what the other kids got. Each child got varying amounts.

" but he shall acknowledge the firstborn, the son of the unloved, by giving him a double portion of all that he has, for he is the firstfruits of his strength. The right of the firstborn is his." Deuteronomy 21:17

Alan Caplin

This is exactly what happened with the prodigal son. He received a share of the inheritance, but the older son who stayed had received **DOUBLE** what the younger son did.

And he said, "There was a man who had two sons. And the younger of them said to his father, 'Father, give me the share of property that is coming to me.' And he divided his property between them. Luke 15:11-12

Elisha very well knew the inheritance structure of Israel, and when Elijah was about to be taken up – Elisha very *intentionally* asked for the inheritance of the first born. Yes. He asked for the *double portion*, the amount that was set aside *specifically* for the first born.

With deliberate intent, Elisha asked Elijah for the double portion or right of the first born which is the **allotment of inheritance given to Jesus!**

It's a ***hard thing,*** but when we <u>see</u> Jesus and the promises of The Lord. When we live from surrender for the benefit of kingdom. When we leave the 99 seeking after the ***ONE.*** When we live from rest and knock on the door of The Holy Spirit for ***others*** ... we too have the right of the first born!

Yes, we are then able to live just as He did and with the same power He had. In *covenant* with Jesus, *you* have the right to the inheritance of the *first born* or *double portion*. You *can* settle for less, you *can* have the inheritance of the 7th or 8th born child, but **you** are a jar of clay awaiting *more* of His treasured oil. You are meant to inherit *all* Jesus has. Friends, seek all that He *is* and be poured out (Phil 2:17).

"But we have this treasure in jars of clay, to show that the surpassing power belongs to God and not to us."
2 Corinthians 4:7

LEAVING THE 99

Universalism and Preterism

"For, speaking loud boasts of folly, they entice by sensual passions of the flesh those who are barely escaping from those who live in error. They promise them freedom, but they themselves are slaves of corruption. For whatever overcomes a person to that he is enslaved." 2 Peter 2:18-19

Often, when people leave *religion* and *legalism* feeling wounded - the end result is false doctrine. They come out so angry at the manipulation and control of religion, that many of these folks find every possible reason to refute all sound teaching. They escape those living in the error of legalism, only to end up selling *false freedom* and becoming a slave of corruption. Yes, many who escape religion are used by darkness to *invent* and *peddle* false teaching.

Universalism and preterism are heretical theologies. Both deny all forms of judgment and steal the near ripe fruit growing from the limbs of the believer. It is impossible to be fully dead to self, to sell out for the gospel, to sit in a place of surrender and selflessness, and to take the kingdom at absolutely any cost ... when everyone is *already* saved.

If the original apostles died for *that* gospel, they were truly lunatics and we shouldn't believe a single word they've written. Any strand of universalism is predicated on the removal of all judgment, specifically final judgment. This is why most, if not all these universalists eventually end up becoming preterists (Jesus already came back in 70 AD).

The only way all can be saved is if Jesus already came back (judged the Jewish people) and He is no longer returning to judge those who are *not* of new spiritual Israel (believers).

Alan Caplin

These 2 doctrines, both universalism and preterism, are flat out anti-christ – they are truly anti-Jesus. In fact, they are akin to a spiritual abortion as life forming in the image of Christ becomes snuffed out ... taking with it all of the fruit forming on the limbs of the baby tree. These false teachings steal purpose, identity, and perpetuate the god of self.

Let's start with universalism (all saved). I was once asked by a friend if I believe in hell. This is my answer:

Short answer. *No.*
Long answer. *Yes.*

The modern view of hell (as a place of eternal judgment) cannot exist because this place hasn't been created yet *(The Lake of Fire)*. Our personal books (of works, lives, deeds, hearts) haven't been opened yet, nor has The Book of Life been opened.

This won't be an answer you've heard before, so please pardon the long explanation.

The original Greek and Hebrew terms:

- The Grave
- Gehenna
- Hades
- Tartarus
- Abraham's Bosom

All refer to ***Sheol***. Sheol is where Jesus went between His death and resurrection to get the keys to eternal death. <u>And</u>, Sheol is *still* the very place where souls are being held today awaiting judgment on the last day.

Sheol has <u>3</u> compartments:

LEAVING THE 99

- **Abraham's Bosom** (emptied when keys obtained)

- **Gehenna/Hades** (those awaiting final judgment; Rich Man & Lazarus account)

- **Tartarus** (Demons, Fallen Angels)

Verses used for above: *Revelation 1:18; Revelation 20:11-15; 1 Peter 3:19-20; 2 Peter 2:4; Luke 16:19-31; and Luke 23:39-43*

Yes, the word "hell" was probably made up by persons of great power to create fear and control ... but ... it doesn't mean that the original words in scripture are wrong.

People will attempt to refute the existence of "hell" as they say ... Jesus was referring to a literal garbage dump when talking about Gehenna (which has been both renamed and branded as hell). Well, **YES**, Jesus **WAS** in fact referring to a literal fiery, smelly, evil garbage dump!

But, our parable and analogy wielding Jesus didn't all of a sudden *stop* speaking in the analogous!!!! Like everything else, Jesus pointed to the literal to make a visual analogy. Jesus certainly wasn't going to talk about our *eternity* and *salvation* with a *literal* example of a trash dump. How does that even make sense?

Every Jewish person was horrified of judgment and eternity (because it was so terribly unclear within the Old Testament scriptures). Having been raised Jewish, I can tell you they worked so hard to be clean and *still* had no fuzzy idea if they were clean or not! Yes. These law-toting Jewish people were so absolutely mortified about "The Book of Life" – that they knew *exactly* what Jesus was talking about!

Alan Caplin

So. Besides a trash dump, what else did **Jesus** say about ***judgment***?

"And as Moses lifted up the serpent in the wilderness, so must the Son of Man be lifted up, that whoever believes in him may have eternal life." John 3:14-15

"Truly, truly, I say to you, whoever hears my word and believes him who sent me has eternal life. He does not come into judgment, but has passed from death to life." John 5:24

"Truly, truly, I say to you, whoever believes has eternal life." John 6:47

"And these (goats) will go away into eternal punishment, but the righteous (sheep) into eternal life." Matthew 25:46 (sheep and goats added for clarity)

What does ***John*** testify to about Jesus?

"Whoever believes in him is not condemned, but whoever does not believe is condemned already, because he has not believed in the name of the only Son of God." John 3:18

"Whoever believes in the Son has eternal life; whoever does not obey the Son shall not see life, but the wrath of God remains on him." John 3:36

"No one who denies the Son has the Father. Whoever confesses the Son has the Father also." 1 John 2:23

"Whoever has the Son has life; whoever does not have the Son of God does not have life." 1 John 5:12

LEAVING THE 99

We cannot wrap our arms around *John 3:16* and at the same time refuse the very sobering reality of *John 3:18*. The same John who was so deeply loved by Jesus, also clearly writes about judgment.

"For God so loved the world, that he gave his only Son, that whoever believes in him should not perish but have eternal life." John 3:16

"Whoever believes in him is not condemned, but whoever does not believe is condemned already, because he has not believed in the name of the only Son of God." John 3:18

Our private rhema (voiced) Jesus will never, ever refute public logos (message) Jesus. Yes, Jesus *is* the covenant (Isaiah 42:6; 49:8), but this covenant must be *entered into* via belief.

For what does the Scripture say? "Abraham believed God, and it was counted to him as righteousness." Romans 4:3

When we realize that hell (The Lake of Fire) hasn't *yet* been created, that means the biblical account of Sheol is still for *today*! Yes. Let's consider the account of Lazarus and The Rich Man - the account Jesus gives where the rich man is suffering in a chasm of flames that cannot *ever* be closed. This *can't* be dismissed as "that's pre-cross" ... this is an account of Sheol which is *still* operational (Luke 16:19-31)!

Friends, I don't teach about hell (Sheol) – because it isn't going to bear much fruit ... not because I don't believe that judgment exists. And, it isn't even relevant to me if eternal judgment is a conscious, experiential thing or not. For The Rich Man, he's been there a *really long time* sweating it out.

Alan Caplin

Paul says that on the "Last Day" there will be a separation - forever shut out from His presence. The temporary (Sheol) will be tossed under judgment into the eternal and forever (Lake of Fire). **AND**, the temporary heaven will be tossed **INTO** the **NEW** heaven (2 Peter 3:13)!

"They will suffer the punishment of eternal destruction, away from the presence of the Lord and from the glory of his might, when he comes on that day to be glorified in his saints, and to be marveled at among all who have believed, because our testimony to you was believed."
2 Thessalonians 1:9-10

The Lord *isn't* there. It can't be good. That's enough for me.

What makes me crazy is that I see people constantly on social media saying that at the end of time every knee will bow in belief and that everyone will be saved. There is no hell, no judgment, and everyone lives happily ever after.

Like everything, the devil twists the word. ***What*** exactly will every tongue confess???

They will confess guilt or innocence!!!

"Turn to me and be saved,
  all the ends of the earth!
  For I am God, and there is no other.
²³ By myself I have sworn;
  from my mouth has gone out in righteousness
  a word that shall not return:
'To me every knee shall bow,
  every tongue shall swear allegiance.'
²⁴ "Only in the LORD, *it shall be said of me,*
  are righteousness and strength;
to him shall come and be *ashamed*

LEAVING THE 99

all who were incensed against him.
*²⁵ In the LORD all the **offspring** of Israel **(believers)**
shall be justified and shall glory."*
Isaiah 45:22-25 **(emphasis and believers added for clarity)**

Every tongue will flat out swear that 'In the Lord alone are righteousness and strength'. This is not a confession of one's belief, this is a confession of **WHO JESUS IS!** Yes, I can confess all day long that Olive Garden is a restaurant and *not* believe the food is good.

This is a courtroom trial. This is a moment where **BY HIS SPIRIT** every person will swear with an account of their heart. Those who descend as the offspring of Jesus Christ (Galatians 4:28), will stand judged guilt free at the cross. But. Those who *"rage against Him"* will be put to shame.

"Turn to me and be saved" (verse 22) – this repentance and turn to The Lord is a *requirement for salvation*!!!!

So. What does Paul actually say in Romans 14:11-12?

for it is written, "As I live, says the Lord, every knee shall bow to me, and every tongue shall confess to God." So then each of us will give an account of himself to God.

Yes. Each of us will give an account of ourselves to God, and we will each acknowledge God is who He says He is!

Friends, there is no way around the Truth that belief from the **HEART** (Romans 10:10) is required for salvation. I'm also going to say something that will be very unpopular.

Many people use **1 Peter 3:18-20** to say that between the death and resurrection of Jesus, that Jesus went to Sheol (hell) to get the keys to death **AND** preached to those who were disobedient in the past. Many use this verse to say that there is a *second chance* of eternal life after death.

I just don't see that. I will supply the verse below, but here is what I believe this verse says.

Remember. The whole book of 1 Peter is in the context of our own suffering in the flesh for the faith. Written as an encouragement to us, this verse is saying that Jesus suffered too. He as the Righteous One suffered for the unrighteous in order to bring them to God. Like us, Jesus was put to death *in the flesh* and is now *alive by the Spirit*. But. In the days of Noah - while building the ark that only saved 8 - Jesus preached life *through* Noah!

Jesus didn't preach to the spirits in Sheol. And as some suggest, Jesus didn't do a victory dance and spike the salvation football in front of these spirits.

- The spirits **NOW** in prison.
- The spirits awaiting judgment.
- The spirits there because of their own disobedience.

They are there because they rejected the message of life from Jesus through Noah and only 8 were saved. **YES**. Jesus preached *through* Noah. And was rejected by all except 7 others.

Read it slowly. Peter and Paul loved to write in run-on sentences - which leaves much treasure for us to find.

*"For Christ also suffered once for sins, the righteous for the unrighteous, that he might bring us to God, being put to death in the flesh but made alive in the spirit, in which he went and proclaimed to the spirits [**now**] in prison, because*

LEAVING THE 99

they formerly did not obey, when God's patience waited in the days of Noah, while the ark was being prepared, in which a few, that is, eight persons, were brought safely through water." 1 Peter 3:18-20 (Emphasis and [**_now_**] added to help people see the difference)

Let's now tackle *preterism*, that Jesus returned in 70 AD. This one is actually super easy to debunk.

People say that they believe what Jesus says, until they just don't like something He said. There is so much social media fodder over 70 AD and the very dangerous belief that Jesus has already returned.

Let's start with what Paul says and end with what Jesus says.

In terms of believers still being here in the earth, Paul calls any talk about a resurrection *already* occurring as "upsetting the faith of some," as "irreverent babble that leads people into more and more **_UNGODLINESS_**," and as "talk that spreads like gangrene."

Folks, gangrene is a ***disease*** that quickly spreads – and causes body tissue to die. Gangrene literally means the death of body parts due to the lack of blood supply and nutrients reaching the limbs.

Paul says to *"depart from the iniquity"* of this teaching because it is so terribly destructive! If this teaching created more and more ungodliness, stole hope, and quickly spread the iniquities of the heart during the time of Paul ... then this teaching does the same destructive stuff to us today! Truly, because of lack of truth, members of the body get sick and die (2 Timothy 2:16-19).

When it comes to His return to earth, I'm going to take what *Jesus* says quite seriously – because Jesus is the One doing the returning!!!

In the parable of the tenants, the owner of a vineyard leases out land and the tenants (Pharisees) failed to produce fruit. When the **OWNER** (The Father) sends multiple servants (the prophets) to get His fruit – the tenants beat, stone, and kill them.

So, the **OWNER** sends His Son, thinking the tenants will have more respect for the Son than the servants that were sent. Yet. The wicked tenants kill the Son too!!!

The parable continues on to say, *"When therefore the owner of the vineyard comes, what will he do to those tenants?" They said to him, "He will put those wretches to a miserable death and let out the vineyard to other tenants who will give him the fruits in their seasons."* Matt 21:40

Jesus tells this parable to the Pharisees, and the Pharisees **KNOW** it's about them. They are about to lose their super prestigious gig ... and in 70 AD the temple fell.

Notice, **WHO** comes to deal with the death and removal of the evil tenants?

Yep - the OWNER, not the SON!

The owner sent the servants, then sent the Son, and then the **OWNER** sent **HIMSELF**! If we want to use this parable in a return scenario, the **FATHER** came to earth in 70 AD – no, not Jesus! Anyone who denies these words of Jesus and continues on with this teaching, is under the influence of a demon. Period.

LEAVING THE 99

Remember, The Father is the judge within the scope of the earth (1 Peter 1:17). Jesus, or more specifically, the word He has spoken will judge on the ***last day*** (John 12:48)!!

The Father – in judgment for both the rejection and murder of the servants and Messiah – tore down the temple. No, it was **NOT** Jesus. The Father Himself had His hand on the judgment of 70 AD.

Paul rebuked preterism as highly dangerous to the body of believers "left" behind and the spoken words of Jesus make this simply implausible. There are many other reasons why this is such terrible teaching, but if what I've written here isn't enough to deter you – then this book about surrender to the voice of The Lord might not be for you.

*"Teach and urge these things. If anyone teaches a different doctrine and **does not agree with the sound words of our Lord Jesus Christ and the teaching that accords with godliness,** he is puffed up with conceit and understands nothing." 1 Timothy 6:3-4* (emphasis added)

Yes. Jesus will return, and He will deal with final judgment of the nations along with the salvation of those waiting on Him (Matthew 25:31-46; Hebrews 9:26-28).

Alan Caplin

Rapture Doctrine

When I came out of Judaism and landed in religion and legalism, at Sunday school they were teaching "rapture" and "tribulation" stuff - I had *zero* idea what they were talking about. But, all I cared about was being able to leave with Jesus before anything bad happened. That's where I was at, and looking back, it was a *heart* problem.

Pre-tribulation rapture teaching is really as dangerous as universalism and preterism because it stunts the growth of the believer. Yes, we are to await/watch for the return of Christ, but far too many of us are looking at this event as *our* rescue ops from The Lord, when *we are the ones who will be doing the rescuing* (Joel Ch 3; Isaiah 61:1-11)!!!

When the Founding Fathers formed this country, pre-tribulation rapture teaching didn't exist. Freedom cost them something ... it cost them their homes, finances, families, and lives. People like George Washington, John Adams, John Hancock, and Patrick Henry had no issue freely laying down their lives for the common good.

Pre-tribulation rapture terminology came about in the late 1800's – around the same time period as the **Industrial Revolution** where we stopped making things by hand. Industry had opened up and people began to travel. Time itself had now become a commodity and people wanted simple, fast, and *easy*! Fast forward to today where we have iphones, fast food, internet, and apps for everything!

We live in a nation where we make little by hand, and we want things done *for* us. Sadly, we have become a nation founded on convenience and no longer on sacrifice!

LEAVING THE 99

Pre-tribulation rapture teaching comes from an encounter in 1830 of Margaret MacDonald in Scotland. She was 15 years old – she had a vision of a *2 stage* return of Christ.

This vision was picked up and spread by preacher John Nelson Darby and began to move far and wide. Based upon the teenager's vision, there was taught to be a period of time *between* the gathering (rapture) and the return.

This 2 stage vision is *correct* that there are 2 portions to the event, but they are **not separate time frames.** Rather, this 2 stage event of the gathering and the return – is on a single day, **<u>The Last Day.</u>**

Yes, on the last day, *(stage 1)* the dead in Christ will arise from their graves and those still alive will be gathering to Jesus in the air. And, *(stage 2)* Jesus will be descending on the clouds in great glory and judgment.

Here is a quick scripture proof that the gathering of the saints to The Lord is on **the last day.**

Now concerning the coming of our Lord Jesus Christ and our being **gathered together** *to him, we ask you, brothers, <u>not to be quickly shaken in mind or alarmed, either by a spirit or a spoken word, or a letter seeming to be from us, to the effect that the</u>* **day of the Lord** *has come. <u>Let no one deceive you</u> in any way. 2 Thess 2:1-3* (emphasis added)

Paul is saying that if anyone tells *you* that Jesus came back and gathered the saints, and that you as a believer are *still* here in the earth ... do not be alarmed!! He says if you are still here, then the **day of The Lord** has **<u>not</u>** yet come, and do **not** be deceived. Aside from the fact that this verse confirms preterism is terrible teaching, it also shows us that the return of Jesus is on **the day of The Lord or the last day.**

In regards to <u>*ALL*</u> believers (both dead and living) Jesus says to us, *"And this is the will of him who sent me, that I should lose nothing of all that he has given me, **but raise it up on the last day.**" John 6:39* (emphasis added)

So, according to Jesus, on *the last day*, both the dead and living rise. Hang with me here, I want to show you how the last day simply isn't split into 2 stages over a period of time like the vision from Scotland in 1830.

Lazarus died and was in a tomb for 4 days. Martha freaks out and tells Jesus, *"I know that he **(Lazarus)** will rise again in the resurrection on the **LAST** day." John 11:24* (emphasis and Lazarus added)

Yet Paul says: *"For since we believe that Jesus died and rose again, even so, through Jesus, God will bring with him those who have fallen asleep. For this we declare to you by a word from the Lord, **that we who are <u>alive</u>, who are left until the coming of the Lord, will <u>not</u> precede those who have fallen asleep.**" 1 Thessalonians 4:14-15* (emphasis added)

The dead rise, and the dead rise **first** on the **last day**. The dead rise **BEFORE** we do. So if Lazarus, Paul, and your Great Grandma Patty are in this group, how is it possible the gathering (rapture) of the saints is **PRIOR** to the dead rising on the last day? The believers who are **alive** cannot leave before the ***dead in Christ*** do!

This is the verse that people want to use to prove that the "rapture" is before any type of *tribulation*.

LEAVING THE 99

"For the Lord himself will descend from heaven with a cry of command, with the voice of an archangel, and with the sound of the trumpet of God. And the dead in Christ will rise first. Then we who are alive, who are left, will be caught up together with them in the clouds to meet the Lord in the air, and so we will always be with the Lord." 1 Thessalonians 4:16-17

But we have to remember that when this was written there weren't chapters, numbers, and headers within the penned letters to the churches. Yes, we have to keep reading the **next** few verses in chapter 5.

The text continues on ... *"Now concerning the times and the seasons, brothers, you have no need to have anything written to you. For you yourselves are fully aware that the **day of the Lord** will come like a thief in the night."* 1 Thessalonians 5:1-2 (emphasis added)

We easily see that the dead rise first, the living rise in the air *after* the dead, and this all happens ... **on the last day.**

I do want to point out that there are those people who would like to compare **1 Thessalonians 4:16-17** with **Matthew 24:30-31** to say there is a split of time between both the gathering and Jesus descending on the clouds in great glory and judgment. However, **both** sets of verses mention 1) a descent, 2) a trumpet, and 3) a gathering of the elect. These two separate accounts from Jesus and Paul are describing the **_same_** exact event ... the **_same_** trumpet blast, **_same_** descent, and **_same_** gathering of the saints on the last day.

"Then will appear in heaven the sign of the Son of Man, and then all the tribes of the earth will mourn, and they will see the Son of Man coming on the clouds of heaven

Alan Caplin

with power and great glory. And he will send out his angels with a loud trumpet call, and they will gather his elect from the four winds, from one end of heaven to the other." Matthew 24:30-31

I once heard a famous teacher say there is no rapture, no gathering, and no meeting the Lord in the air. I've already shown how that's just not true, but I wanted a much better understanding of rapture teaching. So, I asked The Lord for help and I heard, "Follow the trumpets." So I did!!!

When we look closely at the 7 trumpets in Revelation (chapters 8-11) ... it becomes very easy to see that the "gathering" of the saints **cannot** be at *trumpets 1-3* and the "gathering" **cannot** be at *trumpet 7*.

"The fourth angel blew his trumpet, and a third of the sun was struck, and a third of the moon, and a third of the stars, so that a third of their light might be darkened, and a third of the day might be kept from shining, and likewise a third of the night." Revelation 8:12

We see at **trumpet 4** that the celestials are badly shaken. One third of the sun, moon, and stars are struck ... one third of the light on earth is snuffed out.

The text in Matthew 24:29 says, *"Immediately **after the tribulation** of those days (yes, those trumpets of 1-3) the sun will be darkened, and the moon will not give its light, and the stars will fall from heaven, and the powers of the heavens will be shaken."* (Emphasis and trumpets added)

After tribulation, the celestials are then struck. The earth must lose one third of its light **before** the last day comes. Joel confirms this: *"The sun will be turned to darkness and the moon to blood **before** the coming of the great and dreadful day of the Lord." Joel 2:31* (emphasis added)

LEAVING THE 99

The last day **cannot** be trumpets 1-3 because the sky must be darkened **first**. Folks, there is a whole lot of really bad stuff happening in that time period. One just needs to read trumpets 1-3 for clarity on that.

The last day also **cannot** be at trumpet 7.

Jesus says that there are **two** resurrections: one for the *wicked* and one for the *righteous*. Both shall rise. One to life, and one to eternity apart from Jesus.

"Do not marvel at this, for an hour is coming when all who are in the tombs will hear his voice and come out, those who have done good to the resurrection of life, and those who have done evil to the resurrection of judgment." John 5:28-29

Obviously, those in Christ ascend on the last day. The last day isn't the last day of time on the earth ... rather the last day is the second coming of Christ as part of a sequence of great judgments upon the earth. So, after the celestials are badly shaken, after the dead in Christ have risen, after the living have gathered to Jesus in the air ... ***judgment upon the earth rages on with the next set of trumpets.***

Trumpet 7 is the judgment of the **wicked** (Revelation 11:17-18). Since trumpet 7 is the eternal judgment of all the *unbelievers*, and *believers* have been removed, this **cannot** be the timing of the last day.

One other reason that the "gathering" simply cannot be at trumpet 7 is that the 1,000 year reign of the believers with Christ sits *between* trumpets 6 and 7 (Revelation 20:1-6). Those in Christ have *already* exited in the *resurrection of the just* and are now ruling and reigning with Christ on earth for 1,000 years.

Friends, both the teachings of **pre-tribulation** and **post-tribulation** are 100% impossibilities. The gathering has to be between trumpets 4-6. This is *late middle to end* of the tribulation.

Personally, I tend to believe the "exit" for believers is at trumpet 4, and I tend to believe trumpets 5 and 6 are for those *last* remaining *unbelievers*. In my view, trumpets 5-7 occur without *pre-last day believers* in the earth. I say this because immediately *after* trumpet 4 we read, *"Then I looked, and I heard an eagle crying with a loud voice as it flew directly overhead, "Woe, woe, woe to those who dwell on the earth, at the blasts of the other trumpets that the three angels are about to blow!" Revelation 8:13*

It's plausible that we are still here at trumpets 5 and 6, but again, I just don't think that's likely because the terrors of those 2 trumpets are specifically geared to the unbeliever, and the unbeliever *<u>alone</u>*. I tend to believe trumpets 5 and 6 are an intentional weaning by The Lord of those who are left in the earth prior to the millennial reign.

Friends, you *aren't* being rescued. You *are* the rescuer! You are called to **BE** rescue ops. You are called to be a lifeboat. You are called to be Jesus.

"I do not ask that you take them out of the world, but that you keep them from the evil one. They are not of the world, just as I am not of the world. Sanctify them in the truth; your word is truth. As you sent me into the world, so I have sent them into the world." John 17:15-18

As Jesus prayed just before heading to the cross, He prayed that the Father would **NOT** take us out of the world, instead that He'd protect us. Jesus prayed that we'd be sent into the world and mature (or be sanctified) in the Truth.

LEAVING THE 99

Jesus isn't coming to pluck us out of the earth, rather He is maturing us to be just like Him. Jesus isn't desperate for an inferior bride. Jesus isn't going to marry down! Jesus isn't coming back for a shotgun wedding with some mistake He made.

Jesus isn't coming back for an inferior bride, He is coming back for His equal and *greater!* **YOU**, believer, in covenant with Christ are plan A, B, C, and D. Trust in The Lord, and He will *not* fail you!

The world is shaking. And the earth is groaning. Sons and daughters of God, be revealed.

"For I consider that the sufferings of this present time are not worth comparing with the glory that is to be revealed to us. For the creation waits with eager longing for the revealing of the sons of God." Romans 8:18-19

Alan Caplin

Encouragement

Speaking as someone who has "left the 99" many times, leaving the known for the unknown isn't easy. And in that place of both discomfort and ambiguity ... sometimes we *misunderstand* what The Lord's perfect love is and what His perfect love is *not*.

I love to write, and I've written very many things in my maturation journey with The Lord. But, this piece is by far my *favorite* thing that I've ever written! I believe as you walk towards your **"one thing"** these thoughts on perfect love will serve as a great encouragement to you.

Love Rant:

My wife loves my son. So very much.

When my son was younger, my wife **worried** about him being able to tie his shoes on his own at school. So, she got him Velcro sneakers.

Seemed like a good idea.

Well, the kid couldn't tie his shoes on his own until 5th grade! Why? That was when he outgrew all the Velcro shoes at the mall.

Let's just say my kid was embarrassed for a few weeks in 5th grade trying to get his shoes tied.

At some point, love *ceases* to be love. Yes, what we humans see as love - sometimes is really just fear, pride, or selfishness wrapped in a layer of love.

LEAVING THE 99

Good parents expect from their children.
Good parents tell their kids no at times.
Good parents teach and model discipline.
Good parents allow kids to have moments of frustration.
Good parents set both boundaries and limits.
Good parents are able to listen more than they speak.
Good parents allow safe, non-harmful, non-damning, natural consequences as a learning and growing tool.

Much the same.

God's love doesn't enable our poor behavior.
God's love doesn't excuse us from our call.
God's love doesn't mock people.
God's love doesn't exalt ourselves over others.
God's love doesn't place self over kingdom.
God's love doesn't use the word "love" as a weapon.

God's love does correct.
God's love does discipline.
God's love does rebuke.
God's love does endure.
God's love does discern.
God's love does protect.
God's love does find a way.
God's love does hurt and cry with us.
God's love does equip.
God's love does provide.
God's love does say no and not yet.
God's love does honor promises with yes and amen.

Perfect love is able to teach perfect independence.
Perfect love is able to judge and remain perfect.
Perfect love is able to co-labor.
Perfect love is able to trust.
Perfect love is able to form character.

Alan Caplin

Perfect love is able to foster obedience.
Perfect love is able to develop perseverance.
Perfect love is able to find a better way.
Perfect love is able to keep no record of wrongs.
Perfect love is able to honor those you don't like.
Perfect love is able to work through our disappointment.

Yes. God's love will *always* prevail. But just don't expect Him to do things your human way .... and that's for your own growth and benefit as a son or daughter.

He wants us free of self. Free of fear. Free of agenda. Free of sorrow. Free of hurt. Free of the world. Free of our faults and failures. Free of anything and all that comes between us and our purpose in Him.

Thankfully, we can count on His perfect love to **never** be wrapped around fear, pride, or selfishness. But, we can surely count on His love to perfectly strip ourselves of the thorns and thistles that stunt our own growth.

Trees that are lovingly and carefully pruned, will always bear more fruit.

"By this is love perfected with us, so that we may have confidence for the day of judgment, because as he is so also are we in this world. There is no fear in love, but perfect love casts out fear. For fear has to do with punishment, and whoever fears has not been perfected in love. We love because he first loved us." 1 John 4:17-19

LEAVING THE 99

Closing Prayer and Blessing

I didn't *really* begin to read my Bible until I was 45 years old. I began to teach at church, and I wanted to make sure I was teaching what was true. I felt a strong accountability for being as accurate as I could. Then, I began just getting *more and more* curious about how the kingdom worked, I had wanted to know His **ways**!

10 years later, I write this book by *faith*! I have received many of His personal promises, and yet I still *hunger* for so much more that He has specifically promised. I have been living everything I've written in this book, this has *not* been written because it just sounded good!

It's been the most incredible journey!!! God is good!

In the name of Jesus, I bless your walk in The Lord. I bless your leaving the 99. I bless you with the Shalom peace and presence of The Holy Spirit. From your head to your toes I blanket you in the consuming love of Jesus. I release His perfect love over you. I release His favor over you. I speak to the *one* you are headed after and I prepare that person and/or place with the full provision of heaven. I command supernatural provision in all areas to manifest from the unseen realm.

I speak to your body and I command anything that needs healing to be healed *now* by the blood of Jesus. Body and mind be healed. I speak His peace to your heart and mind. I break off all anxiety, fear, shame, hurt, guilt, and doubt.

Alan Caplin

I break off all witchcraft, jealousy, and all hateful things spoken over you. Trauma and spirit of trauma flee now in the name of Jesus. Any and all spirits harassing you, leave now. I break off any and all generational demonic assaults flowing from the iniquity of the heart. Get out, now!

I bless your enemies. I bless those who have mistreated you. I bless those that seek to destroy you. I bless those who didn't understand you. I free them of responsibility, for they know not what they do.

I speak to the heavens, and I release/assign new angels to your path. Angels to bring provision and to prepare your way. Angels to strengthen you, to guide your steps, to lift you so you won't strike your foot on a stone.

I speak to *your* angel, who has been with you since the day you were born. I ask that angel to manifest and to bring new revelation, new hope, and new plans to be downloaded into your heart from heaven. May keys be given to you to unlock the doors of every assignment from The Lord.

I baptize you in the presence of The Lord, and I ask that His Spirit would rest upon you and remain. May you be able to rest in His Truth, and may new giftings open *now* in the name of Jesus.

I send angels ahead of you, and I release the power of The Holy Spirit to be a lamp to your feet.

Bless you, bless you, bless you ... and I thank The Lord for those who have been *awaiting* Christ in you. Thank you, Jesus for those who are reading this, touch them in a fresh way.

Thank you Lord for the gift of being your son.

LEAVING THE 99

Special thanks to my friends Lydia Wright and Stephanie Weir, we did it! Go Jesus!

Alan Caplin

Free Books From Alan

Made in the USA
Monee, IL
16 October 2023

44708521R00085